THE WHOLE WORLD IN HIS HANDS

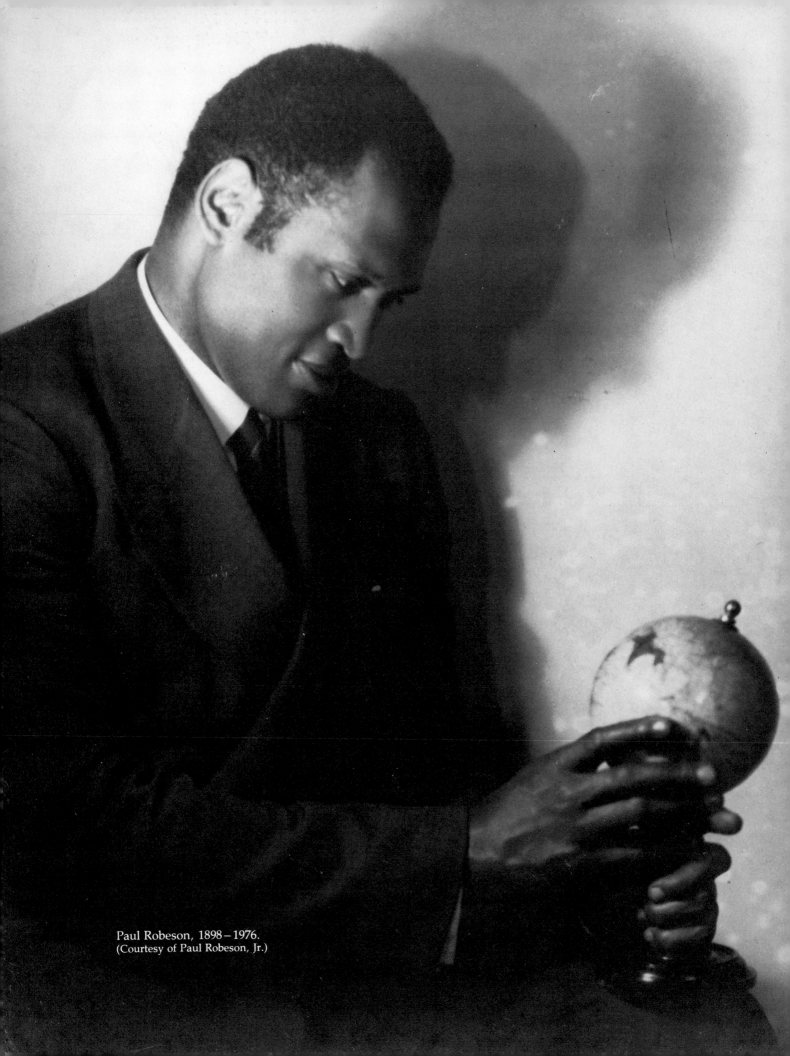

Paul Robeson, 1898–1976.
(Courtesy of Paul Robeson, Jr.)

THE WHOLE WORLD IN HIS HANDS

A Pictorial Biography of Paul Robeson

SUSAN ROBESON

CITADEL PRESS   SECAUCUS, NEW JERSEY

First edition
Copyright © 1981 by Susan Robeson
All rights reserved
Published by Citadel Press
A division of Lyle Stuart Inc.
120 Enterprise Ave., Secaucus, N.J. 07094

In Canada: Musson Book Company
A division of General Publishing Co. Limited
Don Mills, Ontario
Manufactured in the United States of America by
Halliday Lithograph, West Hanover, Mass.

Designed by A. Christopher Simon

LIBRARY OF CONGRESS CATALOGING IN PUBLICATION DATA

Robeson, Susan, 1953–
  The whole world in his hands.

  Includes index.
  1. Robeson, Paul, 1989–1976. 2. Robeson, Susan,
1953–   . 3. Africo-Americans—Biography. I. Title.
E185.97.R63R62   782.1'092'4 [B]   81-6116
ISBN 0-8065-0754-3   AACR2

the images of this book are dedicated to

CHET WASHINGTON

a man in whom the elements have combined to produce
a creative force of splendid artistic, spiritual
and intellectual qualities. . . .

his essence and spirit are a branch
of the Great Tree that is Paul Robeson. . . .

Thank you for your love, dedication and assistance.

ACKNOWLEDGMENTS

My deep gratitude to the Schirmer family for years of hospitality and kindness, for it was during a retreat at their beautiful Cape Cod home that this book first took shape. Grateful acknowledgments go to Julius Lazarus, Morgan Smith, Dorothy Hunton, Anthony Armstrong-Jones, Roger Wood, Lloyd Brown, *Freedomways, The Daily World, The Guardian*, Beauford Smith, Joanna Steichen and Eastman House for permission to use photos from their collections. Heartfelt thanks go to my father, Paul Robeson, Jr., for bringing me together with my publisher Lyle Stuart and for his years of dedication to preserving the Paul Robeson Collection from which so many of the photos in this book come. A special thanks to Freda Diamond for sharing her memories, to Lyle Stuart and the staff at Citadel Press for their faith in me, and to Chris Simon, the designer of this book, for his artistic touch and sensitivity to me and the material. A special note of recognition goes to my grandmother, Eslanda Robeson, for it was she—with her uncanny sense of history—who collected and saved the hundreds of photos and more than 50,000 other items in the Paul Robeson Collection, that have made this book possible.

Several months before death, Philadelphia, 1975.
(Courtesy of Lloyd Brown).

CONTENTS

THE WHOLE WORLD IN HIS HANDS

FAMILY PORTRAIT, New York City, 1957.
(Back left, my mother Marilyn, grandmother, Eslanda
Robeson; father Paul, Jr.; seated front, author; grand-
father Paul; brother David)

PROLOGUE

This is a book of images. The pictures in it are more than photographs. They are the material things of our twentieth-century culture that will become part of my grandfather's immortalization. Image has come to dominate and define the quality of our lives to an overwhelming extent. It is through images that we model how we look and pattern our lifestyles and behavior, shedding old values and taking on new ones. Images are more alive and influential than most realize or admit. So it is that the images of this book are imbued with great meaning and spiritual significance. If one observes them well, looking to their inner side, contemplating all aspects of the frozen moment in time, and compares them to the more established images of their day, one will see, hear, and understand something of Paul Robeson's essence that cannot be written.

I have assembled this book as though making a documentary film, working with several layers. First, the actual images of my grandfather, from his childhood to the last year of his life; second, a narrative consisting of biographical sketches highlighting the significant moments and forces that shaped his life; and third, his own words culled from speeches,

writing, notes, and interviews. I have tried to harmonize these layers in the same way that, as a filmmaker, I would juxtapose image, narration, and other sound, allowing each to tell its own story. The flow of chapters and the grouping of photos within represent the unfolding of a life and a consciousness.

My grandfather was one of the great minds and most accomplished and unique artists the twentieth century has produced. He was also much more:

The first Black man to be named all-American in college football; considered one of the greatest ends in the history of the game

An all-round college athlete, star of baseball, basketball, and track

An all-around academic genius in college at Rutgers University, graduating Phi Beta Kappa and valedictorian of his class

One of the first Blacks to play and star in professional football

The third Black graduate of Columbia Law School

The first Black lawyer to enter one of New York's most prestigious law firm

One of America's greatest concert and interpretive artists

The first concert artist, along with Roland Hayes, to raise Black spirituals to their rightful place of respect, in the best concert halls of the world

The most significant Black actor in America of both stage and screen

The first Black actor to rise to international prominence in film and bring dignity and respect to Black characters

A brilliant scholar of language and world culture, recognized as such by some of the world's most repected historians; he also studied, spoke, and wrote more than twenty languages, including several African languages, Chinese, Russian, and Arabic

An accomplished musicologist

A symbol of excellence on the American stage

The actor who gave the most memorable performance and profound interpretation of Shakespeare's *Othello* in modern times

A model for American youth in his prime

A worldwide symbol of the artist as activist and spokesman for the poor and oppressed in America and throughout the world

An inspiration to the American labor movement

America's first truly Renaissance man—an accomplished singer, actor, activist, athlete, orator, musicologist, and scholar

An international hero

Son of a slave who escaped to freedom at age fifteen

I was born on February 27, 1953, and raised in Harlem during an era dominated by the repressive and hawkish atmosphere of the McCarthy years and the Cold War. I came of age

and first grasped some understanding of my grandfather's greatness during a time when he was under enormous political and personal pressures. From 1950 to 1958, an unofficial but effective ban on Robeson concerts was imposed and his passport was taken away, because of his outspoken political ideas. As a result, my grandfather was forced into inactivity, unable to function as a professional artist in America or abroad. His active, creative life came to a standstill—a devastating situation for any artist, especially an artist of his enormous talents. A curtain of silence was systematically erected, sealing him off from the public eye, and few heard anything more about Paul Robeson. He became a nonperson in his own homeland. Finally, in 1957, after almost a decade, my grandfather broke through the wall of silence, and by 1958 he had reestablished his concert career and won back his passport through a Supreme Court ruling. Triumphant, he left with my grandmother for Europe to fulfill many longstanding invitations.

The seeds of this book were planted in the years that followed as I searched for an understanding of the profound significance of my grandfather's life.

In 1963, when I was ten years old, my grandfather returned amid great controversy, after five years abroad. I watched the media cover and report his return home. Without fail, they characterized it as his return from self-imposed exile, and the public concluded that he had left America many years before, to live in "Communist Russia." The truth is, my grandfather never spent more than a total of two years in the Soviet Union during the entire course of his life.

There was hardly a mention that he had left America after years of persecution, to sing and perform in Europe. His life was made out to be a mysterious and bitter tragedy with sinister overtones. The media portrayed my grandfather as a broken man, returning to the homeland he had rejected and forsaken. They painted an image of a man betrayed by the "Communists," among whom he had sought refuge. Nothing could have been further from the truth, but the media pulled out all stops to perpetuate the false images they had invented for the public mind. I wanted to know why.

Over the next three years, from the ages of eleven to thirteen, I grappled with this contradiction of who I knew my grandfather to be—his ideas, his principles, what he did and said—and how the public perceived him. This especially hit home when I was among my peers. Most knew little or nothing about Paul Robeson. For my own sensibilities, I had to understand the how and why of this paradox of my grandfather's greatness.

During these years I was also grappling with a public school system that assaulted my dignity and intelligence. I was shocked and insulted by the books I was expected to read when I entered the seventh grade in a school for the "intellectually gifted." I was reading *The Autobiography of Malcolm X* and in the midst of exploring my grandfather's library, one of the better and most unusual Black collections in America. It was filled with books about the lives of great men and women down through the ages, histories of Africa by great Black scholars, stories of freedom fighters from all parts of the world, books on African and Chinese languages, music, culture, and philosophy, and the writings of W. E. B. DuBois, Langston Hughes, Richard Wright, and others. Many were signed by the authors with personal inscriptions to my grandfather.

I felt connected to this vast body of knowledge. The stories of the life experiences and sufferings of men and women who helped make history made a deep impression on me. I tried to understand the lessons of their lives and times. I was propelled through hundreds of years and across thousands of miles in my mind's eye, yet never strayed from the root and bond of family. I was inheriting knowledge and learning to see the world and its motive forces through the vision of my grandfather. Unfortunately, all this was not on the seventh-grade curriculum that year.

My life in school was also marked by the shaping of my identity. I was often stunned by the rather warped perceptions of many of the White students, who made up 90 percent of the student body. Many found it hard to believe that I did not try to pass for White, being light enough to do so easily. They considered Black inferior and remained flabbergasted and scornful at my pride in my Blackness. Others expressed their racist opinions about Black people within earshot, and still others saw me as Black and rejected me without question. I had an unusual window on the world, which caused me to reflect on the contradictions of American society and to search history for the keys to understand.

I now felt compelled to explore my grandfather's life in depth and detail, in order to understand his ideas and how he had come to them. I wanted also to understand how his public image had been so viciously distorted.

There was a tiny room in the back of my family's apartment filled with scores of boxes, the contents of which now comprise the Paul Robeson Collection, permanently housed at Howard University. There were more than fifty thousand items—photographs, newspaper clippings, tapes, manuscript writings, correspondence, and even art from places like Africa and Central America. I was especially drawn to the photographs, for they seemed to capture and bring alive every significant moment of my grandfather's life.

I spent hours and days in this tiny, hot room, lost in my explorations. I read hundreds of newspaper accounts of what he had said and done during a forty-year period; I read correspondence between all kinds of personalities and my grandparents; I looked at concert and theater programs and read diaries and speeches. I was filled with a tremendous pride at the profound impact my grandfather had on the world, and I was excited by the vast body of knowledge his life opened up to me.

Around the same time, the fact that my grandfather's father had been a slave exploded in my consciousness. The horror and brutality of slavery became real to me—I could see and feel them in personal terms. I knew my great grandfather to be a man of great dignity and intelligence, and I tried to envision such a man as a slave.

It's difficult to put into words the feelings and emotions that raced through my young being. I felt a deep and lasting pride in my personal heritage and that of my people, in knowing that a man of my great grandfather's caliber had resisted and emerged from slavery to produce a Paul Robeson. Even the most oppressive conditions could not crush the creative genius and beauty of the Black spirit. Yet rage and sadness overwhelmed me. That a society could devise and maintain a system so savage and inhumane as slavery was incomprehensible to me.

The spirituals my grandfather sang suddenly took on new meaning. I learned that many were songs of resistance and their images a secret language to communicate and arrange escape from slavery. I realized what the spirituals meant to my grandfather, and I, too, felt a bond with them.

From an early age, I realized the importance of pride and respect of self and what these do for a young mind—especially when confronted at every turn with the message that one is nothing, comes from nothing, and will no doubt amount to nothing. Many nights I lay awake in bed and cried at how insensitive and cruel the world can be, especially for a young Black child.

The privilege of being Paul Robeson's granddaughter would often overwhelm me. As the years passed, a sense of responsibility to my heritage and my people took shape in me. I had been given to, and in turn, I must give. My life became a search for the answers how.

Though I was exposed to so much, so young, in many ways I was no different from my contemporaries. Like all young people my age, I watched a lot of television. My generation was the first real television generation; we were born, raised, and ripened to maturity with—or rather, by—television. About 1968, when I was fifteen, I became infuriated by the images television was bombarding me with and even more infuriated by what I did not see. There were virtually no images of Black people on television, and what Black images there were showed no dignity or intelligence.

My knowledge of history and my understanding of world events brought me into direct conflict with the media. Herein lay the seeds of my future, unbeknown to me or my family. I sensed how influential the media are, as a powerful merchant of ideas through images. The media shape and control the public mind by manipulating images; yet we don't seem to grasp that it's happening and that we are virtually defenseless. What helped me understand this was a growing realization of the role the media played in relation to my grandfather and the disdain and contempt he developed for the Establishment media. His contempt was born of his experience.

My grandfather stood up at every opportunity and spoke out against the injustices and degradation that Black people experience in America; he embraced the cause of poor and oppressed people wherever they were, no matter what the price or personal sacrifice. He refused to let his success lull him into accommodation; he would "not retreat, not even one thousandth part of one inch." This was an image that the American government found an embarrassing and intolerable threat. Beginning in 1946, when he had reached the pinnacle of fame and fortune the world over, the media began to crucify him, twist his words, distort his image, and then ignore him as though he never existed.

It was unprecedented in the history of America for an artist of his prominence and international stature to be so persecuted. It was what I now call the battle of images—a struggle to feed the public suitable images in order to control and shape their opinions.

A few years later, in 1975, I began to catalog the photos I had discovered more than a decade earlier in that tiny, hot room in the back of our apartment. I came full circle. The realization of the tremendous power of my grandfather's image and the compelling need to reawaken that image in the public mind struck me full force. I wanted to share the path of discovery I had journeyed . . . and so this book of images was born.

Meanwhile, my life and work came to focus around images: I embarked on a career in television. In looking back over the course of my life thus far, I realize how great an influence that medium has played in making me the person I am today. As Paul Robeson's granddaughter, I had the unique opportunity to see first hand how the media can manipulate, distort, and create false images. It was an unusual experience to watch this process unfold. It taught me that the media, which our society thinks of as unblemished sources of truth and accurate information, can be the most vicious purveyors of untruths.

My life experiences have instilled within me a profound respect for the sacredness and inviolability of trust and have imbued me with a deep inner understanding of principle and, above all, the meaning of living one's life according to these values. They are the lost qualities of our society, without which we will continue to grope in darkness.

I was taught by example—the best teacher—and discovered through my grandfather the power of family and ancestors. An unshakable strength exists when the cycle of inheritance remains unbroken and historical truths are reexperienced through family bonds, generation after generation. Family is the root and foundation of civilization . . . and the vehicle for creating lasting change.

Somewhere in each and every one of us a ray of my grandfather's light shines. Find that light and let it shine. It will guide you to truth, impel you to stand up for justice, and instill within you the lost virtue of principle. You will be unalterably changed. That is the challenge and offering of his life. He, too, is a part of your heritage . . . but you must first lay claim.

New York City   *1980*

Rutgers University, junior year, 1918. (Courtesy of Paul Robeson, Jr.)

1
BEGINNINGS

My grandfather Paul Robeson was born in Princeton, New Jersey, on April 9, 1898, the son of an escaped slave. He grew up in Princeton with his three older brothers, William, Reeve, and Ben, and his sister, Marian, nourished by the extraordinary strength and courage of parents who were steeled by the cruel realities of slave society. In 1904, when Paul was six years old, tragedy struck with the death of his mother, Maria Louisa Bustill Robeson. Nearly blind, she was burned to death when a coal from the household stove accidentally set fire to her dress.

A few months after his mother's death, Paul's father, the Reverend William Drew Robeson, lost the ministry of his Princeton church. Devastated, but with dignity and strength still intact, Reverend Robeson moved his family to nearby Westfield and then to Somerville, New Jersey, where Paul finished elementary school and high school, graduating in 1914.

Many of Paul's early years were filled with poverty, and only an extended family including aunts, uncles, and cousins, many just arrived from the cotton and tobacco fields of North Carolina, helped keep the family to-

gether. But the dignity and quiet strength of Reverend Robeson were the bedrock of sustenance for his family, especially young Paul.

Princeton, in those days, had the demeanor of an old southern town, with its ruling White aristocracy, rigid class lines, and deeply embedded racism. But Reverend Robeson, never one to scrape or bow, raised himself to be among the most respected and honored men of the community in the eyes of both Blacks and Whites. He had been born a slave in Robersonville in Martin County, North Carolina, on July 27, 1845. He escaped as a young man of fifteen and headed north to freedom via the Underground Railway. Within several years, my great grandfather had educated himself in the finest classical tradition and graduated from Lincoln University's divinity school.

In less than a decade Paul's father had freed himself from bondage and scaled the heights of knowledge. He was a man of penetrating dignity and fierce determination. Above all, he was a true man of principle, and this quality, along with unbending courage and an intense pride in the Black race, was instilled in Paul from an early age.

My grandfather once said, in this regard, "I

19

marvel that there is no hint of servility in my father's makeup. Just as in youth he had refused to remain a slave, so in all the years of his manhood he disdained to be an Uncle Tom. From him we learned, and never doubted it, that the Negro was in every way the equal of the white man. And we fiercely resolved to prove it."[1]

Paul's education began at home in the bosom of his family. His mother, a highly educated schoolteacher, came from a long line of free Black ancestors, as well as Quaker and Native American (Indian) ancestors. But it was Reverend Robeson who oversaw the family's intellectual and moral development. He also possessed a deep and passionate speaking voice and trained Paul from an early age in the skills of public oratory. Sunday afternoons the family would often gather, taking instruction from one another and sharing in the art of self-education.

At sixteen, Paul graduated with honors from Somerville High School, and in 1915 he won an academic scholarship to Rutgers University in New Jersey. Paul was the third Black person ever to attend Rutgers and the only one during his four years there. Life on campus was permeated with the racist attitudes typical of the era, and these attitudes confronted Paul at every turn. But Reverend Robeson had prepared his son well, and Paul excelled in everything. He won the major oratorical contests four years in a row; he gained the distinction of winning America's highest scholastic honor, the Phi Beta Kappa key, in his junior year; and he was twice named end on the All-America football team, making him the first Black All-American in Rutgers history.

Paul was also the star catcher on the Rutgers baseball team and played center on the basketball team. He earned letters in football, baseball, track, and basketball, breaking down every imaginable barrier with his athletic prowess and academic genius. Paul was also a member of the Rutgers Glee Club, but his participation was restricted by the racist mores of the time. Social events and dances were a major part of Glee Club activities, and

Paul was barred from these. But in his years at Rutgers, Paul's quiet dignity and personal integrity shamed many a Rutgers student.

In 1919 Paul graduated, valedictorian of his class. It was a proud moment, but a deep sadness filled Paul's life—his father had died earlier that year, at the age of seventy-three. Now alone, Paul moved to Harlem and entered Columbia Law School in 1920. He had chosen law as the best vehicle to channel his talents and help uplift the Black race. To make ends meet, Paul played professional football on weekends and coached basketball. And then, in 1921, he met and married Eslanda Cardozo Goode, a brilliant and beautiful woman—the first Black analytical chemist working at Columbia Medical Center in New York.

The early years of Paul's life laid the foundation for certain character traits that have come to symbolize his life and that assumed legendary proportions in the 1950's, during the years of his persecution. His father had instilled in him a sense of principle that was inviolable. Stand up for what you believe in, he was taught, no matter what the price or the consequences. Never back down if you know you are right. A matter of principle is sacred, and if you forfeit your principles for the sake of personal advancement or convenience, you have compromised your dignity and sold your soul. A human being can commit no greater damage to himself or herself.

This is one of the most precious gifts my grandfather gave me. To search for the truth and make it manifest in my life, no matter how much at odds with society the truth put me—this was one of the few maxims that permeated my home as I was growing up. It is a part of my being for which I am eternally grateful. It is the kind of value that is difficult to acquire; rather it must be a reflex, a way of being that necessitates no special thought to act upon.

Fate, more than anything else, seemed to guide Paul to the world of theater. If he had theatrical aspirations, he kept them well hidden or felt that practicing law was more important. Twice during his years at Columbia

Somerville Elementary School, 1910. *(Paul is in the second row, fourth from right.)* (Courtesy of Paul Robeson, Jr.)

Somerville High School football team, 1913. *(Paul is in the second row, fourth from left.)* (Courtesy of Paul Robeson, Jr.)

Somerville High School Baseball team, 1914. *(Paul is in the first row, second from right.)* (Courtesy of Paul Robeson, Jr.)

Rutgers University, 1918. (Courtesy of Rutgers University Library.)

Somerville High School football team, 1913. *(Paul is in the second row, second from right.)* (Courtesy of Paul Robeson, Jr.)

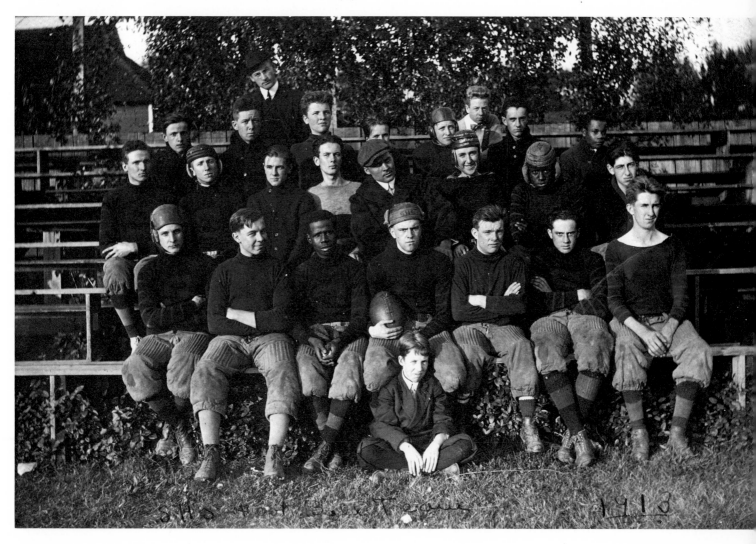

23

Rutgers University basketball team, 1917.
(Courtesy of Paul Robeson, Jr.)

Rutgers University football team, 1917.
(Courtesy of Paul Robeson, Jr.)

24

Rutgers versus Naval Reserve, Ebbets Field, 1917. (Courtesy of Paul Robeson, Jr.)

Rutgers University football team, star players, 1918. (Courtesy of Paul Robeson, Jr.)

Phi Beta Kappa Society, Rutgers University, 1919. (Courtesy of Paul Robeson, Jr.)

Rutgers University, senior year, 1919.
(Courtesy of *Freedomways*.)

We of the younger generation especially must feel a sacred call to that which lies before us. I go out to do my little part in helping my untutored brother. We of this less-favored race realized that our future lies chiefly in our own hands. On ourselves alone will depend the preservation of our liberties and the transmission of them in their integrity to those who will come after us. And we are struggling on, attempting to show that knowledge can be obtained under difficulties; that poverty may give place to affluence; that obscurity is not an absolute bar to distinction and that a way is open to welfare and happiness to all who will follow the way with resolution and wisdom; that neither the old-time slavery, nor continued prejudice need extinguish self-respect, crush manly ambition, or paralyze effort; that no power outside of himself can prevent man from sustaining an honorable character and a useful relation to his day and generation. We know that neither institutions nor friends can make a race stand unless it has strength in its own foundation; that races like individuals must stand or fall by their own merit; that to fully succeed they must practice the virtues of self-reliance, self-respect, industry, perseverance, and economy.[2]

Valedictorian speech to Rutgers University
graduating class, 1919.

Columbia University Law School, graduating class, 1923. (Courtesy of Paul Robeson, Jr.)

Voodoo, London, 1922. (Courtesy of Paul Robeson, Jr.)

Voodoo, London, 1922. (Courtesy of Paul Robeson, Jr.)

On board ship returning from London to complete law school after appearing in *Voodoo*, 1922. (Courtesy of *Photo World*.)

At this time I was an aspiring lawyer, believing that to succeed would help raise my people, the Black people of the world. Theater and concerts were furthest from my mind; this trip was just a lark. Instead of waiting on tables in hotels to earn money, I was being paid twenty pounds or so a week for expenses to walk on a stage, say a few lines, sing a song or two. Just too good for words.[3]

Law School, Paul was drawn to the stage. First, in the spring of 1922, he played the role of Simon in the Harlem YMCA's revival of *Simon the Cyrenian*. The play focused on the day of Jesus' crucifixion. Simon, an African leader of slave rebellions, played by Paul, is summoned before Jesus and arrives sword in hand. Simon has sworn to lead Egypt to freedom from Roman oppression but is deterred by the words of Jesus: "Put up the sword. For they that take the sword shall perish with the sword. . . . Do not resist evil." The play closed with Simon bearing Jesus' cross.

There were no reviews of Paul's first stage appearance, and *Simon the Cyrenian* seemed to make little impression on him. However, at Eslanda's invitation, two men from the Provincetown Theatre were present opening night. Greatly impressed, they offered Paul the title role in *The Emperor Jones*, a new play by Eugene O'Neill. Paul refused the offer, unaware of the pivotal role the Provincetown Theatre and Eugene O'Neill would soon play in his life.

Paul still seemed determined to make a career of law. One month passed, and Paul was again enticed into appearing on stage—this time in London. Augustin Duncan, brother of dancer Isadora Duncan, had been impressed by Paul's performance at the Harlem YMCA. He convinced Paul to appear in a play he was directing called *Taboo*, opposite the famous English actress Margaret Wycherly. *Taboo* opened in New York and then toured England during the summer of 1922. The English production was renamed *Voodoo* and directed by Mrs. Patrick Campbell, who played the female lead and was the first major influence on Paul's career. As Paul later described it,

Voodoo was loosely constructed. . . . It started on a southern plantation and had a throwback to Africa. . . . In the play I fell asleep and in my dreams returned to the land of my forebearers. I sang "Go Down Moses" as I lapsed into my dream, and I was startled during the opening performance to hear Mrs. Pat whispering off-stage, for all the theater to hear, "Another song, another!" So I would wake up hurriedly and find another spiritual. In all my supposedly heavy dramatic scenes Mrs. Pat would nudge me, and off I'd go singing! . . . The audience seemed to love my singing.[4]

Paul returned to New York at the end of the summer and completed his degree at Columbia Law School. After graduating, he worked for several months in one of New York's most prestigious law firms but quit after realizing there would be no end to the degradation and racial insults. A Black lawyer, in those days, was unheard of. Now Paul's real interest turned to the theater.

In 1924, letter of introduction in hand, Paul sought out Eugene O'Neill, who immediately decided to cast Paul in the lead role of Jim in his new play, *All God's Chillun Got Wings*. The production became enveloped in a raging controversy. In the play's final scene, Jim—a Black lawyer played by Paul—is kissed by his wife, a White woman who hardly equals his station in life. Announcement of the production was greeted with widespread hysteria. Ku Klux Klan death threats came from as far away as Georgia and as nearby as Long Island. The Hearst newspaper chain initiated a vicious campaign against the play, and the mayor of New York publicly proclaimed his opposition to the production.

As controversy raged around *All God's Chillun Got Wings* even before it opened, Eugene O'Neill decided to mount a revival of *The Emperor Jones*. This time O'Neill chose Paul to play the title role over Charles Gilpin, the top Black actor of the day, who first made the role of Emperor Jones famous.

The Emperor Jones opened on May 6, 1924, at the Provincetown Theatre in New York to great critical acclaim. When the curtain fell on the final act, according to one major New York reviewer, Paul was called back out "by men and women who rose to their feet and applauded. When the ache in their arms stopped their hands, they used their voices, shouted meaningless words, gave hoarse throaty cries. . . . the ovation was for Robeson, for his emotional strength, for his superb acting."[5] After the successful opening of *The Emperor Jones*, Paul finally opened in *All God's Chillun Got Wings*. Reviews of this play were mixed, though Paul's reception was generally favorable; however, it closed after a short run. *The Emperor Jones* had a longer run than *All God's Chillun,* and when it closed in New York, it reopened in London, with my grandfather in the lead.

Paul returned to New York from London in the fall of 1925. Fate again took hold and pointed him in a new direction, this time toward a career as a concert artist. During his days at Columbia Law School, Paul had done some professional singing, though with no thought of making it a career. Eubie Blake had discovered Paul in Harlem in 1922, before his stage appearances at the Provincetown Theatre, and coaxed him into appearing in his new show, *Shuffle Along,* at Harlem's Cotton Club. Paul did several performances but thought nothing more of it.

Paul's appearance in *The Emperor Jones* really precipitated his singing career. A scene in the play called for him to exit whistling. Never able to whistle, Paul sang a spiritual. The majesty of his voice struck the audience like thunder. Soon after, Paul bumped into Lawrence Brown by chance on a Harlem street corner. Brown was Roland Hayes's accompanist and among the best arrangers and historians of Black folk music. Paul and Larry had met briefly in London in 1922, when Paul was appearing in *Voodoo,* but they had not seen each other since. They had dinner that night with friends.

After dinner, Paul sang a few songs impromptu, with Larry accompanying on the piano. They electrified the gathering. Jimmy Light, director at the Provincetown Theatre, was there. Light was so excited that he begged Paul and Larry to consider giving a recital together. Within three weeks a concert was organized at the Greenwich Village Theatre for May 19, 1925. A veritable who's who of New York society packed the tiny theater, and the next day a prominent New York music critic wrote,

All those who listened last night to the first concert in this country made entirely of Negro music . . . may have been present at a turning point, one of those thin points in time in which a star is born and not yet visible—the first appearance of this folk wealth to be made without deference or apology. Paul Robeson's voice is difficult to describe. It is a voice in which deep bells ring.[6]

It was decided that Paul and Larry should launch a concert tour. Essie quit her job as a laboratory technician in the summer of 1925 and became their manager. For the next four years, Paul and Larry toured the length and breadth of America with phenomenal success. Always, Paul would explain that the spirituals he sang

portray the hopes of our people who faced the hardships of slavery . . . They sang to forget the chains and misery. The sorrow will one day turn to joy. All that breaks the heart and oppresses the soul will one day give place to peace and understanding, and every man will be free. That is the interpretation of a true Negro spiritual.[7]

Together, Paul and Larry raised the folk music of Afro-America—a music of pain and sorrow, and of resistance and struggle as well—to its rightful place in the best concert halls of America.

When I first suggested singing Negro spirituals for English audiences, a few years ago, I was laughed at. How could these utterly simple, indeed, almost savage songs interest the most sophisticated audiences in the world? I was asked. And yet I have found response amongst this very audience to the simple, direct emotional appeal of Negro spirituals. These songs are to Negro culture what the works of the great poets are to English culture: they are the soul of the race made manifest. . . . But the sufferings he has undergone have left an indelible mark on the Negro's soul, and at the present stage he suffers from an inferiority complex which finds its compensation in a desire to imitate the white man and his ways; but I am convinced that in this direction there is neither fulfilment nor peace for the Negro.

In 1928, the musical *Show Boat,* by Jerome Kern and Oscar Hammerstein, catapulted an already famous Paul Robeson to even greater heights. The show's principal song, "Ol' Man River," was written with Paul in mind. Over the years—with a few changes—he forged it into a song of resistance that came to symbolize Paul Robeson the artist as a freedom fighter.

The opening of *Show Boat* in London was an event much awaited by the British public. London's most sophisticated and cultured audience packed the Drury Lane Theatre, and hundreds more were turned away. Paul's performance brought the house down. The usually discreet and subdued British went wild over Paul's voice and his towering, but serenely dignified presence. Overnight, he became one of England's most popular and sought-after artists. Ironically, the American embassy in London, usually quite hospitable to White American artists, chose to ignore Paul.

Paul and Essie decided to settle in London, finding it far more conducive to Paul's artistic development than America, where racism was more stifling. In London, they were exposed to the most prominent and cultured members of English society as well as many of the most outspoken radicals and political thinkers of that era. They shared numerous evenings of discussion about art, culture, and world events with people like George Bernard Shaw, H. G. Wells, Gertrude Stein, and many others. Paul's social and political development was taking shape. He began to give deeper thought to his role in the world and his aim in life.

In 1930, announcements appeared in the press that Paul Robeson would star in a London production of *Othello*. No Black actor had played Shakespeare's *Othello* since Ira Aldridge in the 1860s. Paul approached it with the discipline and mind of a scholar. He studied not only *Othello* and Shakespeare's other works, but the English language of Shakespeare's time. Paul studied phonetics and listened to countless records to improve his pronunciation. He commented in a *New York Times* interview,

I have read virtually everything of Shakespeare's. Now that I know the English people and really understand what their country means to them, now that I am in touch with the English spirit, I feel I can play *Othello*. It is the same with music. People ask me why I do not sing Schubert and Brahms. Perhaps I shall one day, but not before I have lived in Germany."[8]

Paul related to *Othello* as no White actor could. His interpretation was revolutionary, yet true to Shakespeare. Paul viewed Othello as a Black man of noble ancestry, alone in a hostile and alien White society. Feeling his honor betrayed, Othello kills—not out of jealousy, but from the deeper roots of cultural and racial integrity. The interpretation surprised the British public; it sent shock waves through America.

Many profound changes occurred within and around Paul during the next decade in London. A cultural awareness and spirituality of great depth were emerging that would guide him for the remainder of his life. These elements were deeply rooted in the bond Paul felt with Africa, both historically and culturally, and a Black consciousness emerged that embraced Black as beautiful and rejected the aping of White cultural values. He warned against the alienation, the psychological scars, and the destruction of their souls that would overcome Black people if they did not take pride in their African cultural identity. This led Paul to research the importance of cultural integrity to human existence. He made profound explorations into the origins of African languages and music and discovered their affinity with Eastern cultures, leading him to conclude that African peoples are more Eastern than Western in values and culture. He felt that blindly following Western values would destroy the souls of Black people. The great British historian Arnold Toynbee hailed Paul's writings and philosophy as profoundly critical in understanding world history and the evolution of society.

In 1934, Paul made his first trip to the Soviet Union, at the invitation of Sergei Eisenstein, the great Russian film director. It was an experience that touched deep chords in Paul, one he would never forget.

He passed through Germany first, traveling by train with Essie and Marie Seton, an English biographer. Hitler was rising to power then, and Nazi stormtroopers were everywhere. The few hours they spent in Germany, waiting for the connecting train to Moscow, made an ominous impression on Paul. In the train station, an ugly scene unfolded so reminiscent of a lynch mob that Paul felt as if he were in America, in the Deep South. Since his wife was very light skinned, Nazi stormtroopers guarding the train station thought he was traveling with German women. They formed a tight circle and began to close in on Paul and Marie Seton while Essie was at the other end of the platform searching for their luggage.

Paul, understanding German and the racial epithets the SS troopers snarled back and forth, literally braced himself to fight to the death. At that moment the train pulled up, and miraculously, they escaped without incident. Never had Paul felt so close to death. There, on the train to Moscow, a profound realization of the deep-rooted evil of fascism and its many faces overwhelmed Paul, and he vowed to fight it for the rest of his life.

Paul's welcome in the Soviet Union was a vivid contrast—he had had no idea of his tremendous popularity there. But more significantly, Paul was treated with full human dignity. He found no traces of superiority or racism in the ways people related to him. It was a liberating experience, and the sensation touched Paul's inner core. He spoke perfect, fluent Russian, having studied it for the past two years, and met with many Russians from all walks of life. He returned to London with a great love for the Soviet people and a deep interest in their new national experiment, socialism.

Paul continued his concert tours throughout the English provinces with great success, but one thing had changed. He now sang in the cheaper, popular halls at the lowest ticket prices, sometimes giving three performances a day. Never before had a concert artist of such prominence and stature done so. It was considered undignified, but for Paul it meant he could reach the common working people.

By 1937, war raged in Spain, a kind of dress rehearsal for World War II. Fascists in Spain, with the help of Mussolini and Hitler, were fighting to overthrow the popularly elected government of Spain. The Spanish Civil War became another turning point in Paul's life. He cut short a second trip to Moscow to participate in a huge meeting in London's Albert Hall for the Spanish Loyalists. His appearance on stage was greeted by a deafening roar. Through his music, Paul had come to symbolize the artist dedicated to the cause of freedom. He made a brief but moving speech and then sang "Ol' Man River," by then a Robeson classic. He changed the words for the first time, transforming it from a song of despair to one of resistance. Instead of singing:

Darkies all work on de Mississippi,
Darkies all work while de White folks play,
Pullin' dem boats from de dawn till sunset,
Gittin' no rest till de judgment day. . . .

Tote that barge and lift that bale,
Git a little drunk and ya lands in jail.
I gits weary and sick of tryin',
I'm tired of livin' and scared of dyin',
But Ol' Man River, he just keeps rollin' along.

Paul sang:

There's an old man called the Mississippi,
That's the ol' man I don't like to be.
What does he care if the world's got troubles?
What does he care if the world ain't free? . . .

Tote that barge, lift that bale,
You show a little grit an' you lands in jail.
I keeps laughin' instead of cryin';
I must keep fightin' until I'm dyin',
And Ol' Man River, he just keeps rollin' along.

A few months later, my grandparents were on their way to Spain at the height of the civil war there. Paul sang to the front-line Loyalist troops, which included volunteers from America and all over Europe. He traveled with Essie to the front lines at Madrid and Barcelona, where they experienced some of the worst bombings of the war. At Teruel, the guns on both sides were stilled while Paul sang. Paul emerged a living legend and a worldwide symbol of the artist as freedom fighter.

The story of Spain is a part of my childhood memories going back as far as I can remember. We had a tradition in the family of telling "grandfather stories." Weekend car trips were usually the setting. I was fascinated and exhilarated by the stories of his experiences; I felt that I was connected to the world he touched because his blood ran through my veins. History and world events became a part of my life through his life. They weren't the cold, hard facts you read about in a book or newspaper; they were moments I could picture in my mind's eye and comprehend through my grandfather.

The Spanish Civil War became a moment in history very vivid and alive to me, and the story of my grandfather's trip to Spain was one I asked to hear over and over. Somehow, as a child, I realized what an extraordinary moment in history and in his life it was, and it came to symbolize for me his incredible spirit and ability to penetrate the hearts and minds of people all over the world.

Not only Spain, but the entire decade of the 1930s, was a turning point in my grandfather's development. It's an era that I have recently rediscovered in all its complexities and one that few have taken proper notice of. The 1930s were a time of tremendous intellectual, cultural, and spiritual expansion for my grandfather. During this time he also developed insights into the spiritual and cultural development of the world. The philosophies

he developed in the 1930s penetrate to the core of the dilemma that Western man is faced with today, that is, how to extricate himself from the social monsters of his own creation—the alienation and destruction so characteristic of Western civilization in modern times.

My Grandfather's studies led him to conclude that a split occurred in the psyche of Western man during the Age of Reason, a split that led him to develop science and technology at the expense of art and spirituality. He killed the spiritual essence of life and ever since has been blindly groping in the dark for the key to life. The results are manifest in the destruction, decadence, and inhumanity that seem to go along with Western man today.

My grandfather was also deeply involved in the study of African languages and the ancient musical sources of Africa and the Third World. He discovered a remarkable affinity between African and Chinese cultures. He found the links in music, through the pentatonic scale—a five-tone scale characteristic of both Chinese and African traditional music—and he discovered it in languages, for both Chinese and African languages are based on changes of tone and inflection to give new meanings to words. Further, he discovered that there is a universal body of music, also based on the pentatonic scale.

His curiosity about the amazing similarity between the traditional folk songs of Wales and Afro-American spirituals sparked this, along with the discovery that Gregorian chants from Europe sounded remarkably similar to ancient African chants. He found that all ancient music from around the world is part of a common body of music based on a common means of expression—the pentatonic scale.

These discoveries, arrived at through his own research, provided the historical and cultural foundation for my grandfather's dedication to universal brotherhood and world peace.

38

Chorus of *Shuffle Along*, by Eubie Blake and Noble Sissle. Cotton Club, Harlem, 1922.
(Courtesy of Paul Robeson, Jr.)

I've corralled a young fellow with considerable experience, wonderful presence and voice, full of ambition and a damn fine man personally with real brains—not a "ham." This guy deserves his chance, and I don't believe he'll lose his head if he makes a hit—as surely he will, for he's read the play for me and I'm sure he'll be bigger than Gilpin was even at the start.[9]

Eugene O'Neill
1924

With playwright Eugene O'Neill (*center*) and Essie, 1920s. (Courtesy of Paul Robeson, Jr.)

All God's Chillun Got Wings, Provincetown Playhouse, 1924. (Courtesy of Paul Robeson, Jr.)

The Emperor Jones, London, 1925. (Courtesy of BBC Hulton Picture Library.)

When my London audiences watch me play the Emperor Jones . . .

They see a modern Negro roll up the centuries and reveal primeval man. . . . One does not need a very long racial memory to lose oneself in such a part. . . . As I act civilization falls away from me. My plight becomes real; the horrors, terrible facts. I feel the terror of the slave mart, the degradation of man bought and sold into slavery.[10]

London Interview
1925

London, 1925. (Courtesy of Paul Robeson, Jr.)

In studio of sculptor Antonio Salemme, 1926. (Courtesy of Paul Robeson, Jr.)

Nude study, New York, 1926. (Photo by Nicholas Murray/Courtesy of Paul Robeson, Jr.)

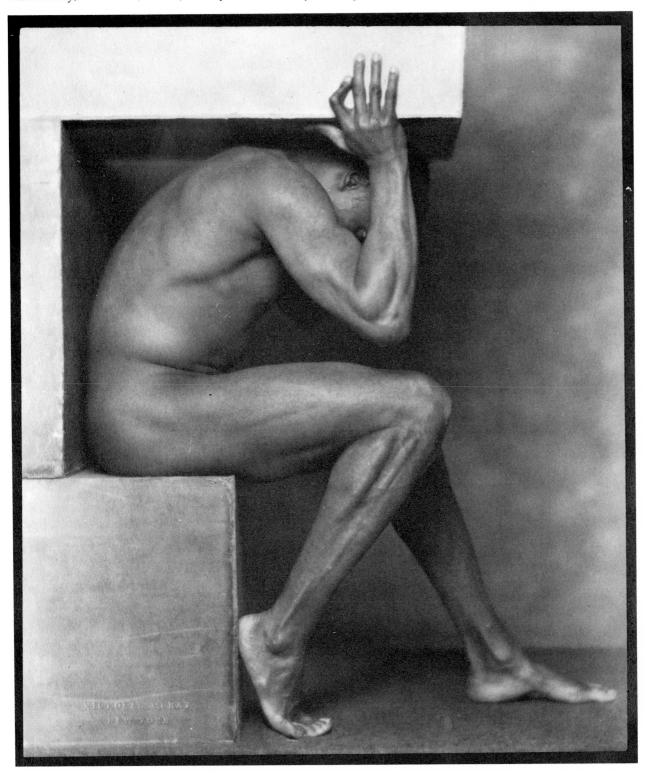

London, 1925. (Courtesy of Paul Robeson, Jr.)

London, 1925. (Courtesy of Paul Robeson, Jr.)

(Opposite page)
Nude study, New York, 1926. (Photo by Nicholas Murray/Courtesy of Paul Robeson, Jr.)

"Realizing quite rightly that a nation is ultimately judged not by its might but by its culture, the Negro has set out to try to absorb Western arts. What he has not understood is that culture cannot be put on from the outside. A certain artificial grace may be achieved by such means, but only at the cost of strangling the natural creative impulses. That is too big a price to pay, and the race that pays it will never be an influential people."[11]

London home, 1928. (Courtesy of Paul Robeson, Jr.)

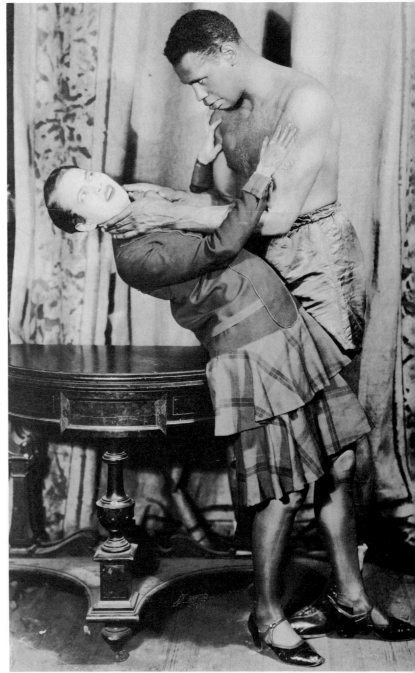

London, 1928. (Courtesy of Paul Robeson, Jr.)

With Fredi Washington in Eugene O'Neill's Broadway production of *Black Boy*, New York, 1926. (Courtesy of Paul Robeson, Jr.)

We who start on this rather untrodden way need all the support and encouragement we can possibly get. I approach the future in a happy and rather adventuresome spirit, for it is within my power to make this unknown trail a somewhat beaten path.[12]

London Interview
1924

London, 1928. (Courtesy of Paul Robeson, Jr.)

Show Boat, Drury Lane Theatre, London, 1928. (Courtesy of Paul Robeson, Jr.)

Show Boat, Drury Lane Theatre, London, 1928. (Courtesy of Paul Robeson, Jr.)

50

Show Boat, with Alberta Hunter *(fourth from left)*, Drury Lane Theatre, London, 1928. (Courtesy of Paul Robeson, Jr.)

51

Cast party, opening night of *Show Boat*, Drury Lane Theatre, London, 1928. (Courtesy of Paul Robeson, Jr.)

"Othello in the Venice of that time was in practically the same position as a coloured man in America today." [13]

London Interview
1930

Othello, Savoy Theatre, London, 1930. (Courtesy of Paul Robeson, Jr.)

With Peggy Ashcroft as Desdemona in *Othello*, Savoy Theatre, London, 1930. (Courtesy of Paul Robeson, Jr.)

54

Listening to the latest-model Marconiphone radio, London, 1931. (Courtesy of BBC Hulton Picture Library.)

"My ancestors in Africa reckoned sound of major importance; they were all great talkers, great orators, and where writing was unknown, folk tales and an oral tradition kept the ears rather than the eyes sharpened. I am the same way. I always hear, I seldom see. I hear my way through the world."[14]

Studying a Russian song in preparation for Albert Hall concert, London, 1931. (Courtesy of BBC Hulton Picture Library.)

I "discovered" Africa in London. That discovery—back in the twenties—profoundly influenced my life. Like most of Africa's children in America I had known little about the land of our fathers. But in England, where my career as an actor and singer took me, I came to know many Africans. Some of their names are now known to the world—Azikiwe, and Nkrumah, and Kenyatta, who has just been jailed for his leadership of the liberation struggle in Kenya.

Many of these Africans were students, and I spent many hours talking with them and taking part in their activities at the West African Students Union building. Somehow they think of me as one of them; they took pride in my successes, and they made Mrs. Robeson and me honorary members of the union. . . .

I now felt as one with my African friends. . . . I learned that along with the towering achievements of the cultures in ancient Greece and China there stood the culture of Africa, unseen and denied by the imperialist looters of Africa's material wealth. . . .

I came to see the root sources of my own people's culture especially in our music, which is still the richest and most healthy in America . . . and I came to learn of the remarkable kinship between African and Chinese culture.[15]

With African students, London, 1936. (Courtesy of Paul Robeson, Jr.)

Presentation of honorary membership to Paul and Eslanda in West African Students Union, London, 1936. (Courtesy of Paul Robeson, Jr.)

I hesitated to come; I listened to what everybody had to say but I didn't think this would be any different from any other place. But—maybe you'll understand—I feel like a human being for the first time since I grew up. Here I am not a Negro but a human being. . . . Here, for the first time in my life, I walk in full human dignity.[16]

Comment to Russian filmmaker Sergei Eisenstein in Moscow, 1934

Greeting Russian film director Sergei Eisenstein during Paul's first visit to the Soviet Union, 1934. (Courtesy of SovFoto.)

Moscow concert, with accompanist Larry Brown, 1936. (Courtesy of Paul Robeson, Jr.)

With Sergei Eisenstein and friends during first trip to
Soviet Union, 1934. (Courtesy of Paul Robeson, Jr.)

Moscow, 1934. (Courtesy of Paul Robeson, Jr.)

War-torn streets of Madrid, 1937. (Photo by Eslanda Robeson/Courtesy of Paul Robeson, Jr.)

With members of the International Brigade, Madrid, 1937. (Photo by Eslanda Robeson/Courtesy of Paul Robeson, Jr.)

The artist must elect to fight for freedom or for slavery. I have made my choice. I had no alternative. The history of the capitalist era is characterized by the degradation of my people: despoiled of their lands, their culture destroyed . . . denied equal protection of the law, and deprived their rightful place in the respect of their fellows.

Not through blind faith or coercion, but conscious of my course, I take my place with you.[17]

Speech at London Rally for Spanish Loyalists
1937

With Black American volunteer in International Brigade, Madrid, 1937. (Photo by Eslanda Robeson/Courtesy of Paul Robeson, Jr.)

Singing to troops of the International Brigade, front lines of Madrid during Spanish Civil War, 1937. (Photo by Eslanda Robeson/Courtesy of Paul Robeson, Jr.)

Jericho (Dark Sands), Egypt, 1936. (Courtesy of Paul Robeson, Jr.)

2
SCREEN IMAGES

*In my music, my plays, my films I want always to carry
this central idea: to be African.
    Multitudes of men have died for less worthy ideals;
it is even more eminently worth living for.*[1]

My grandfather's journey through the world of cinema was a search to express the inner cultural core of Black people. He saw film as more than an art form for entertainment; he saw it as a tool for removing racial and cultural stereotypes. He sought to instill pride and dignity in Black people through the power of screen images. His consciousness of images and their political overtones unfolded during the seven years, from 1932 to 1939, in which he actively worked in the industry.

At the beginning, he was less critical of the roles he accepted, believing that so long as he played a leading character that did not overtly demean Black culture, he would make a significant contribution. As he developed into an artist with a strong sense of political and social responsibilities and as he acquired greater insight into the workings of the film industry, he became increasingly critical of the films he associated himself with.

There were times when his image on the screen was deliberately manipulated, undermining his original intent. By 1937, his disappointment at the inability of producers to allow him to portray Black characters with intelligence, strength, and dignity led him to refuse any further work in the commercial film industry. He rejected scores of lucrative offers, as a matter of principle.

Paul was the first Black person in film history to demand and receive the right to final approval of his films—known as "final cut." He was also the first in the industry to refuse work under segregated conditions and stipulated in all his contracts that he would not work in the South. Above all, he was the first to truly dignify African culture and the essential Africanness of Black Americans on the screen. He was a loner in the film industry during its formative years, and he was constrained by the limitations of others who had little comprehension of how to utilize his enormous creative abilities and intellect.

My grandfather challenged the inherent racism of the film industry to its foundations, for which he paid a price perhaps greater than that of any artist in American history. He did so proudly, as a matter of principle and with no regrets.

BODY AND SOUL

Oscar Micheaux   New York,   1924

Body and Soul was Paul's film debut. It was a silent film made when Paul was on the threshold of a career in the theater, during the days of his involvement with Eugene O'Neill and the Provincetown Players in Greenwich Village. *Body and Soul*'s release came back to back with Paul's first major stage performances in 1924, in *All God's Chillun Got Wings* and *The Emperor Jones.*

Body and Soul was a landmark in the annals of Black cinema. It is probably the one film that best represents Oscar Micheaux, the most prolific Black filmmaker of the 1920s, who broke significantly with the aping of White cinema values that predominated in Black films. It is even more significant, historically, because almost all Oscar Micheaux's other films have been lost or destroyed.

The plot of *Body and Soul* is confusing, perhaps the result of the New York Board of Censorship, which forced Micheaux to reedit the film at least once. But it does reflect a racial consciousness and insight into contradictions within the Black community. Paul is the focal point as a preacher who possesses a dual na-

ture—the quintessence of virtue and the depths of opportunism.

BORDERLINE

Kenneth McPherson   Switzerland,   1930

Kenneth McPherson was the editor of the well-known European film journal *Close-up* and deeply involved in the avant-garde world of film theory and technique. *Borderline* reflected McPherson's overriding concern with the more abstract ideas of film theory, and as a result the story of *Borderline* was experimental, with its plot often overstated or underdeveloped. The film was symbolically set in a borderline town, somewhere in Europe, where the paths of two couples cross—one White, the other Black. *Borderline* focuses on the racial and interpersonal conflicts that result from their interaction within the confines of a small town. Essie starred with Paul in the role of his wife.

Borderline was privately shown and received little critical notice. It got more attention for its experimental techniques—unusual camera angles and editing. The film was most significant in that it gave starring roles to Black performers, and Blacks were portrayed in human, social terms. A British reviewer commented at the time that "*Borderline* is an attempt . . . to treat the Negro as a sensitive and intelligent being."[2] It also stimulated public interest in seeing Paul act and sing in a "talkie."

Body and Soul, New York, 1922.

On location during filming of *Borderline*, Swiss Alps, 1930. (Courtesy of Paul Robeson, Jr.)

Body and Soul, New York, 1922.

With director Kenneth MacPherson and Eslanda during filming of *Borderline*, Swiss Alps, 1930. (Courtesy of Paul Robeson, Jr.)

THE EMPEROR JONES

United Artists Release NEW YORK, 1933

The Emperor Jones was Paul's first major commercial film. Its success gave him prominence as a major artist in the world of cinema, and in the Black community it heightened his already heroic stature. *The Emperor Jones* was revolutionary in its own time. It projected an image of the Black man that had never been shown on the commercial screen, a man of strength and dignity—with "brains and nerve," as the character himself puts it—and the pride to stand up to the White man as an equal, if not a superior. His dreams are not those, so typical of the era, of a cowed or happy-go-lucky musical Negro, but dreams of attaining the heights of power and respect, challenging the premise that a Black could not do this in the White man's world. These images were taboo, for they challenged, on the screen, the rationale of White supremacy.

The genesis of *The Emperor Jones* came in 1930, in the earliest days of the talkie in Hollywood. Eugene O'Neill was developing a screen version for his original play. He went so far as to write Essie to inform her of his work, and he insisted that he would not sell the screen version unless Paul again played the title role. For some reason, O'Neill never produced the film. *The Emperor Jones* was eventually made by two young independent producers, John Krimsky and Gifford Cochran. They commissioned DuBose Heyward, the author of *Porgy,* to adapt *The Emperor Jones* for the screen. Heyward did so, with Eugene O'Neill's approval, and Dudley Murphy was brought in as director and J. Rosamond Johnson as musical director.

The first half of the film traces the emergence and exploits of Brutus Jones, a young Black who gets the proverbial chance to make it big in the city, with a job as a Pullman porter. During his train runs, Brutus is introduced to the fast night life of Harlem and succumbs to its attractions—especially the beautiful girlfriend of a friend, played by Fredi Washington. Jones is transformed from a naïve country boy into a sharp womanizer and

worldly-wise man. But he soon finds himself imprisoned on a southern chain gang, convicted of the accidental murder of his best friend, whom he discovered cheating during a crap game in a Harlem club.

The chain-gang scenes made bold social commentary, as well as displaying Robeson's splendid physique and voice. One scene caused so much controversy that it was cut and removed before the film went into distribution and has never been seen in the United States. The scene showed Paul defying and then killing a White prison guard who tried to force him to beat a fellow Black prisoner who was caught escaping. Never before had a Black been shown killing a White on the screen. America could not tolerate any such images of resistance.

After escaping, Brutus Jones makes his way with great determination and ingenuity to a small Caribbean island. This is where the original O'Neill play began. Brutus is captured by the island's tyrannical Black ruler but escapes a sure death when a British trader buys him for a paltry sum. Brutus uses his intelligence, drawing the island people close to him. He takes over the White trader's business and then overthrows the island's dictator. Brutus becomes the Emperor Jones. The film builds to another level of character exposition and explores the corrupting influences of power and the price it exacts from those who yield to it.

The Emperor Jones opened in New York in the fall of 1933, downtown at the Rivoli and uptown in Harlem at the Roosevelt. The downtown box-office receipts were not outstanding, but in Harlem the film grossed more than ten thousand dollars in the first week, with more than two hundred thousand Black people packing the theater and the film often playing to standing-room-only crowds. The scenes of Robeson confronting the White man and resisting instilled in these audiences a pride and dignity they yearned for but could not find elsewhere on the screen.

The reviews were generally favorable. The critics proclaimed *The Emperor Jones* an artistic success, though it was not a commercial one.

The Emperor Jones, 1933. (Photo by Edward Steichen/ Courtesy of Joanna Steichen.)

With Fredi Washington, *The Emperor Jones*, New York, 1933. (Courtesy of Paul Robeson, Jr.)

With Essie en route to New York to begin filming *The Emperor Jones*, London, 1933. (Courtesy of Julius Lazarus Collection.)

The Emperor Jones, New York, 1933. (Courtesy of Paul Robeson, Jr.)

The Emperor Jones, New York, 1933. (Courtesy of BBC Hulton Picture Library.)

With Dudley Diggs in *The Emperor Jones*,
New York, 1933. (Courtesy of Paul Robeson,
Jr.)

With Nina Mae McKinney and Joan
Gardner, Paul's co-stars in *Sanders of the
River*, London, 1934. (Courtesy of Paul
Robeson, Jr.)

A few reviews were critical, but there was virtual unanimity in praising Paul's performance. Several weeks after the opening, the Black press began to voice some misgivings about the image of Black people projected by Paul. One reviewer stated that his characterization "perpetuated a stereotype of blacks as morally corrupt, superstitious and easily discouraged after momentary triumph has passed."[3] But these reviewers seemed to have missed the mark, perhaps not realizing the deeper levels of human character that O'Neill was developing—of a personality unraveling from the abuse of power.

But Paul was a genuine hero to the Black community and so highly respected that even these criticisms were delicately posed. Paul remained publicly silent. He was at the beginning of a process from which he would emerge, a few years later, with the most principled, sensitive, and revolutionary consciousness of his day concerning the Black image on the screen.

Studio portrait, London, 1934. (Courtesy of Paul Robeson, Jr.)

With Nina Mae McKinney, *Sanders of the River*, London, 1934. (Courtesy of Paul Robeson, Jr.)

On location with Jomo Kenyatta, *Sanders of the River*, London, 1934. (Courtesy of Paul Robeson, Jr.)

For the first time since I began acting, I feel that that I've found my place in the world, that there's something out of my own culture which I can express and perhaps help to preserve. . . . I have found out now that the African natives had a definite culture a long way beyond the culture of the Stone Age . . . an integrated thing, which is still unspoilt by western influence. . . . I think the Americans will be amazed to find how many of the modern dance steps are relics of an African heritage.[4]

SANDERS OF THE RIVER

London Films   LONDON, 1935

In the summer of 1934, Paul was in London immersed in profound explorations, through language and music, into the roots of African culture. He was searching for the universal core of human existence. He was also concerned with conditions of life in colonized Africa and began to associate with many of the leading figures in British politics, as well as the many African and Asian students studying in London. Some, like Kwame Nkrumah, Jomo Kenyatta, and Jawaharlal Nehru, later returned to their countries to lead them to independence.

Paul's deep involvement with African culture led him to accept an offer in the summer of 1934 from British film producer Alexander Korda to play the lead role of Bosambo in *Sanders of the River*. What intrigued Paul, and hooked him, was director Zoltan Korda's plan to incorporate documentary material filmed in Africa. Korda sent a fifteen-man crew into remote areas of Africa; they traveled more than fifteen thousand miles in four months, making an unprecedented visual record of traditional African dances and ceremonies. These scenes were to be used as background footage and interwoven with studio scenes. Traditional African music was also recorded as the background for the musical score.

Paul set to work with great excitement, concentrating his energies on developing the character of Bosambo with credibility and dignity. Paul felt that if he could portray an African leader with cultural integrity and accuracy he would be making a contribution in helping people—especially Black people—to understand the roots of African culture. Paul came to realize that a solid cultural core is the only foundation upon which a race of people can stand. *Sanders of the River* became a turning point in my grandfather's life . . . and a decision he came to regret deeply.

Paul began filming *Sanders of the River* in 1934. At the same time the Soviet film director Sergei Eisenstein was developing a feature film on the life of Toussaint L'Ouverture, the Haitian liberator. Eisenstein's interest in Toussaint stemmed from his trip to Mexico to film *Que Viva Mexico* in 1931. There he discovered and read *Black Napoleon*, a biography of Toussaint. By the time Eisenstein returned to Moscow he felt that Toussaint represented the emergence of the oppressed genius of Black people. Having always wanted to do a film with Robeson, Eisenstein decided that *Black Napoleon* was the film to do. So Eisenstein invited Paul and Essie to come to Moscow. This was my grandfather's first trip to the Soviet Union. Marie Seton, a close friend of Eisenstein's and later Paul's biographer, accompanied Paul and Essie.

When Paul returned to London from Moscow, the Kordas asked him to film several retakes of scenes from *Sanders of the River*. He discovered that the thrust of the film and his character had changed significantly. Bosambo, the African leader, had been made into a loyal servant of his British "masters." The film was now a rationalization for the white man's rule over Africa. Paul later explained in an interview that "the twist in the picture which was favorable to English imperialism was accomplished during the cutting of the picture, after it was filmed. I had no idea it would have such a turn after I acted in it. Moreover, when it was shown at its premiere in London, and I saw what it was, I was called to the stage, and in protest refused to perform. Since that time I have refused to play in three films offered me by that same producer. . . . I was roped into the picture because I wanted to portray the culture of the African people."[5]

Paul was so disillusioned with the film that he attempted, unsuccessfully, to buy the rights and all the prints, to prevent its distribution.

SHOW BOAT

Universal Studios   HOLLYWOOD, 1935

Show Boat was Paul's first film for a major Hollywood studio. It was also the one film of his career that he was least motivated to make. When first offered the part, Paul turned it down. He and my grandmother were living in London, having made it their home since Paul's opening there in 1928 in the stage musical of *Show Boat*. Paul was having phenomenal success with his concert tours throughout the English provinces. He was also still deeply immersed in studies of African and folk cultures. Life in London was exciting and challenging, filled with an intellectual and cultural stimulation that Paul craved and knew he could not find in America.

Universal commissioned Jerome Kern and Oscar Hammerstein, authors of the original *Show Boat*, to write a version for the screen. They immediately wrote to Paul in London, wanting only him to play the role of Joe in the film version. Essie, by then handling most of Paul's affairs, wrote back asking for such a high fee that both she and Paul were convinced Universal would refuse. To their surprise, Universal agreed.

In the fall of 1935, Paul and Essie left for the United States. They stopped in Milwaukee and then Seattle, where Paul did several concerts, and then headed for Hollywood. In less than two months, the filming of *Show Boat* was complete and Paul was back in London for a concert series in the winter of 1936.

When *Show Boat* opened it was greeted by rave reviews in both the United States and Europe. Paul was singled out for lavish praise. One reviewer wrote, "For superb recording and dramatic richness, the honors must go to 'Ol' Man River,' sung more stirringly than ever by Robeson."[6] Almost every critic cited Paul's singing alone as worth the admission price. Many lamented that Paul's part was too small.

SONG OF FREEDOM

Hammer-British Lion　　London, 1936

By 1936, Paul decided he had a much better chance in England than in America of portraying Black people in a dignified and culturally accurate manner. "In America," he said, "the color question is too acute, and prejudice is rampant. A serious Negro artist stands very little chance there."[7]

In the summer of 1936, a few months before *Show Boat* opened, Paul signed a contract to appear in a new British production called *Song of Freedom*, starring opposite Elizabeth Welch. By this time, Paul was extremely critical about the roles he accepted, but he agreed to *Song of Freedom* based on the story line. It centers around Zinga, a Black dockworker in England, whose singing and deep bass voice attract the interest of a great opera impresario. He takes Zinga under his wing, and Zinga soon rises to great fame as an international opera star.

Quite by accident, Zinga discovers that he is of royal descent and should be an African king. He wears a medallion passed on from father to son in his family, and an old anthropologist reveals to him that the medallion is proof of his royal birth. Even before his discovery, Zinga has longed to know the story of his past. He feels out of place in England and is convinced that Africa is his spiritual homeland. After the discovery of his ancestry, Zinga leaves his lucrative operatic career to return to Africa. His dream is to uplift his people by combining the positive aspects of western technology with the best of traditional African ways.

The production called for a film crew to travel through west Africa to shoot documentry scenes of traditional dances and ceremonies for background scenes. This, of course, excited Paul, but he had learned from bitter experience how easily producers could manipulate his image. Paul demanded and won a contract that gave him final cut.

Song of Freedom was a significant film for Paul. "I want to disillusion the world of the idea that the Negro is either a stupid fellow or, as the Hollywood superfilms show him, a superstitious savage under the spell of witch doctors,"[8] Paul declared at a press conference shortly before the film was released. For Paul, *Song of Freedom* accomplished this, and he described it at the time as "the first film to give a true picture of many aspects of the life of the

Sanders of the River, London, 1934. (Courtesy of Paul Robeson, Jr.)

With James Whale, director of *Show Boat*, Hollywood, 1935. (Courtesy of Paul Robeson, Jr.)

Opening night of *Show Boat* in London, Leicester Square Theatre, 1936. (Courtesy of BBC Hulton Picture Library.)

With Jerome Kern and Oscar Hammerstein II. (Courtesy of Rutgers University Library.)

78   World premiere at London's largest theater, 1936. (Courtesy of Paul Robeson, Jr.)

Show Boat, Hollywood, 1935. (Courtesy of Paul Robeson, Jr.)

colored man in the West. Hitherto on the screen, he has been caricatured or presented only as a comedy character. This film shows him as a real man."[9]

Most of the critics agreed with Paul, but *Song of Freedom* was not a commercial success. The film was buried and hardly seen thereafter. The most significant accolade came fourteen years later, in 1950. The film was shown in Accra, Ghana, to open the annual celebration of Ghana's independence party. The ceremonies were presided over by Kwame Nkrumah, Paul's friend of twenty years earlier, who was soon to become the first prime minister of independent Ghana.

With Elizabeth Welch in *Song of Freedom,* London, 1936. (Courtesy of Paul Robeson, Jr.)

Song of Freedom, London, 1936. (Courtesy of Paul Robeson, Jr.)

Song of Freedom, London, 1936. (Courtesy of Paul Robeson, Jr.)

Song of Freedom, London, 1936. (Courtesy of Paul Robeson, Jr.)

KING SOLOMON'S MINES

Gaumont-British   LONDON / SOUTH
AFRICA, 1937

King Solomon's Mines was based on the classic novel by H. Rider Haggard. It had a central character who discovers that he is a dispossesed African king. When he returns to his people, he goes through an intense struggle to overcome their fear and mistrust.

The film was a lavish production, using documentary film shot on location in Africa. Again, it was the storyline and documentary elements that appealed to my grandfather. And to his delight, the production required that he be tutored in Efik to prepare for the role. During these studies Paul discovered the remarkable similarity in inflection and rhythm between Efik and Chinese. This confirmed Paul's developing philosophy of the kinship between African and Chinese cultures.

The reviews were rather restrained, and many criticized *King Solomon's Mines* as over-romanticized. The Black press reacted favorably, noting with great pleasure that Paul had made changes where the film tended to perpetuate the usual stereotype of Africans as bloodthirsty and powerless before the White man. Still lacking, however, was truly potent dramatic and musical material for Paul to sink his teeth into.

JERICHO (DARK SANDS)

Capitol Films   LONDON / EGYPT, 1937

Jericho was Paul's most forceful film in terms of Black images. Its images speak of resistance to injustice by any means necessary, identification with Africa, the use of skills and knowledge from the West to benefit Africa, the foundations and qualities of positive leadership, and Pan-Arab national unity. *Jericho's* ending is positive, projecting success, power, and happiness in the image of a Black man of courage, intelligence, honor, and self-sacrifice.

The film opens on board an American troop ship transporting soldiers to Europe during World War I. The ship is torpedoed, and a large group of soldiers is trapped belowdecks. Jericho Jackson, played by Paul, is a medical student turned soldier. Defying the orders of a panic-stricken White officer to return above deck, he miraculously saves the trapped men from death. In the process, Jericho accidentally kills the officer when the latter tries to force Jericho to obey his order to abandon the men.

Despite his heroism Jericho is court-martialed for refusing an order. Feeling justice betrayed, he executes a bold escape. Captain Mack, a White officer played by Henry Wilcoxon, is held responsible for the escape and court-martialed. Meanwhile, Jericho has escaped by boat and drifted to the coast of north Africa. He wanders through the Sahara Desert, where he encounters the Tuareg people and endears himself to them by using his western skills and medical know-how to heal their sick. Jericho eventually marries and raises a family among the Tuareg. (Paul's wife in the film, Princess Kouka, was an actual princess discovered on location in an African village.) Jericho soon becomes the respected and beloved leader of the Tuareg.

Every year, the Taureg and other nations of the Sahara make a trek across thousands of miles of desert for their annual supply of salt. The trek is traditionally marred by warring among the Arab nations. Jericho proposes to his people that they unite all the nations and make the trek a joint effort that benefits everyone. With the agreement of the Tuareg council of elders, Jericho leads the Tuareg on their annual trek. They are forced to resort to arms to carry out the plan for unity, and Jericho leads his people in victorious battle.

Meanwhile, the salt trek has attracted an anthropological film crew. When they return to London with their exclusive documentary footage, it's shown in the major theaters. Captain Mack, who has vowed to capture Jericho and exonerate himself, spots Jericho in the salt-trek films. Mack tracks Jericho down among the Tuareg but relents in his plan of capture when he sees the good Jericho has done for his people. Captain Mack flies off, but his plane crashes in the desert, killing him.

Paul considered *Jericho* his best film to date, in part because he was successful in changing the ending. The original script ended with Captain Mack capitalizing on Jericho's weakness and homesickness; he convinces Jericho to return to the States, face trial, and clear the captain's name. They leave together by plane but crash in the desert. Jericho, fatally wounded, dies trying to save Captain Mack. With his last words he begs Captain Mack to "tell them that I was coming home." A far cry in imagery and meaning from the ending Robeson inserted.

King Solomon's Mines, London, 1937. (Courtesy of Paul Robeson, Jr.)

With Roland Young and Sir Cedric Hardwicke in *King Solomon's Mines,* London, 1937. (Courtesy of Paul Robeson, Jr.)

On the set of *King Solomon's Mines* with Eslanda, London, 1937. (Courtesy of Paul Robeson, Jr.)

En route to Egypt for filming of *Jericho* with co-stars Henry Wilcoxon, Princess Kouka, and Essie, Marseilles, 1937. (Courtesy of Paul Robeson, Jr.)

With co-star Princess Kouka on opening night of *Jericho*, London, 1937. (Courtesy of United Press International.)

At the Giza pyramids in Egypt, with Wallace Ford and Henry Wilcoxon during filming of *Jericho*, 1937. (Courtesy of Paul Robeson, Jr.)

With Henry Wilcoxon and others, *Jericho*, Egypt, 1937. (Courtesy of Paul Robeson, Jr.)

Jericho, Egypt, 1937. (Courtesy of Paul Robeson, Jr.)

With Princess Kouka, *Jericho*, Egypt, 1937. (Courtesy of Paul Robeson, Jr.)

(Opposite page) Jericho, Egypt, 1937. (Courtesy of Paul Robeson, Jr.)

BIG FELLA

British Lion Studios   LONDON, 1937

Big Fella was based on the novel *Banjo*, by
Claude McKay, a noted Black writer of the
Harlem Renaissance. It was set on the docks
of Marseilles, France, and its characters were
the denizens of the docks and its accompanying street life. *Big Fella's* hero, played by Paul,
was Banjo, a worldly-wise but honest dockworker. The unfolding of his integrity and
deep human values form the crux of the
movie. Elizabeth Welch played opposite Paul
as a café singer in love with him. Larry Brown,
my grandfather's accompanist, had a small
role, as he had in *Jericho*, and Eslanda also had
a part, for which she received excellent critical
notice—so much so, that after *Big Fella*, Essie
screen tested in Hollywood for the role of Pilar
in Hemingway's *For Whom the Bell Tolls*.

Big Fella was received with excellent reviews. It was praised for the sensitivity of
character it enabled Paul to develop, the musical score, which featured both Paul and Elizabeth Welch, and the plot, which reviewers
mentioned enabled Paul to use his "tremendous histrionic ability."

With Elizabeth Welch in *Big Fella*, London,
1938. (Courtesy of Paul Robeson, Jr.)

With Essie, Edward Ashby, and Larry Brown,
Big Fella, London, 1938. (Courtesy of Paul Robeson, Jr.)

With Essie, *Big Fella,* London, 1938. (Courtesy of Paul Robeson, Jr.)

With Larry Brown (Paul's accompanist) and others, *Big Fella,* London, 1938. (Courtesy of Paul Robeson, Jr.)

Proud Valley, Wales, 1939. (Courtesy of Paul Robeson, Jr.)

Proud Valley, Wales, 1939. (Courtesy of Paul Robeson, Jr.)

I find I cannot portray the life nor express the living hopes and aspirations of the struggling people from which I come.[10]

London Interview
1937

Films make me into some cheap turn. . . . You bet they will never let me play a part in a film in which a Negro is on top.[11]

London Interview
1938

I thought I could do something for the Negro race in the films: show the truth about them — and about other people too. I used to do my part and go away feeling satisfied. Thought everything was okay. Well, it wasn't. Things were twisted and changed — distorted. They didn't mean the same.

That made me think things out. It made me more conscious politically.

One man can't face the film companies. They represent about the biggest aggregate of finance capital in the world: That's why they make their films that way. So no more films for me.[12]

London Interview
1937

92

As David Goliath in *Proud Valley,* Wales, 1939.
(Courtesy of Paul Robeson, Jr.)

PROUD VALLEY

Ealing Studios   WALES, 1939

For two years my grandfather refused roles from major film studios, both British and American. Finally, in 1939, he agreed to appear in an independently produced film about the coal miners of Wales. Paul announced to the press that in *Proud Valley* he would "depict the Negro as he really is—not the caricature he is always represented to be on the screen."[13]

Proud Valley was originally conceived to document the harsh realities of the Welsh coal miner's life. It was filmed on location in Rhondda Valley, the heart of Welsh coal country, and many scenes were shot inside the homes of local miners. Paul's character, David Goliath, was based on the true story of a Black American miner from West Virginia who makes his way to England, where he works on the docks, and then drifts to Wales when massive unemployment hits England.

Paul is the center of action. In the film, his magnificent voice draws the Welsh miners and enables him to share in their rich cultural life. As David Goliath, Paul shares the trials and tribulations of the miners' lives and helps them organize a movement for better working conditions. In the end, Goliath sacrifices his life in the mines to save his fellow workers.

The Welsh people were great lovers of my grandfather and his music. They knew of him from his earliest concert tours in Europe in the 1920s. The Welsh are a struggling people with music in their souls, and they felt a deep bond with the sufferings and hopes expressed in the spirituals Paul sang. He, in turn, was amazed to feel a kinship with the traditional folk music of the Welsh.

Proud Valley is the film that my grandfather, in retrospect, felt satisfied him most, both politically and artistically. The Black press at the time agreed: "Hollywood has never produced a picture in which a colored actor or actress has been cast as Robeson is in Proud Valley.

. . . Millions of movie-goers . . . have been waiting to see a colored man cast as a man."[14] The image of Paul's character in *Proud Valley* was revolutionary at the time, for it projected the Black working man as a true hero with the greatest of human and social values.

Proud Valley, Wales, 1939. (Courtesy of Paul Robeson, Jr.)

TALES OF MANHATTAN

20th Century-Fox   HOLLYWOOD, 1942

By the time *Proud Valley* opened, World War II had begun, and my grandfather was back in America, compelled to return by an overwhelming sense of responsibility to share the struggles of his people at home. For three more years, he refused enticing offers from Hollywood and Broadway. One producer offered to make Paul a millionaire if he would only let the producer control Paul's public image—that is, what Paul would say and what he would not say. Finally, in 1942, my grandfather made one final attempt to come to terms with Hollywood: He agreed to appear in *Tales of Manhattan*, a Hollywood spectacle with some of the biggest stars of the day, including Ginger Rogers, Henry Fonda, Cesar Romero, Rita Hayworth, Edward G. Robinson, Charles Laughton, and Ethel Waters.

Tales of Manhattan consisted of a series of vignettes tied together by the travels of an overcoat stuffed with thousands of dollars and its impact on the lives of those who come to possess it. The coat eventually falls from an airplane and is discovered by a southern sharecropper and his wife, played by my grandfather and Ethel Waters. The dramatic conflict unfolds in the clash of ideas over how to use the money. Paul argues for communal sharing to build economic independence, while Eddie Anderson, playing a comic preacher, maneuvers and schemes to the most opportunistic tune, to undermine Paul's attempts to foster independence.

My grandfather deeply regretted having ever made *Tales of Manhattan*. "It was the same old thing, the Negro solving his problem by singing his way to glory," he explained to the press. "This is very offensive to my people. It makes the Negro childlike and innocent and is in the old plantation tradition." Paul stated publicly that he "wouldn't blame any Negro for picketing it."[15] He had hoped that in the course of the filming, he could change much of the film's content. The representation of the deplorable living conditions of Black sharecroppers had attracted Paul to the film. Some reviewers did recognize a subtle indictment of the brutal realities of the sharecropping system, but Paul remained thoroughly dissatisfied. He went so far as to attempt to buy up all the prints so he could take it out of distribution, as he had tried to do with *Sanders of the River*, but the producers refused.

With Ethel Waters and production team, *Tales of Manhattan*, Hollywood, 1942. (Courtesy of Paul Robeson, Jr.)

3
FAMILY
AND CANDID
MOMENTS

My paternal grandmother, Eslanda Cardozo Goode Robeson, known to her family and friends as Essie, was born on December 12, 1896, in Washington, D.C. Her father died when she was six years old. Her mother took the family—Essie and her two brothers—to New York City, where Mrs. Goode hoped to earn a better living and educate her children in integrated schools.

My grandmother was of a notable background, of which she was quite proud. Her grandfather was Frances Lewis Cardozo, a free Black born in the early 1800s, who rose to become a prominent figure in South Carolina politics during Reconstruction. He became South Carolina's first Black secretary of the treasury. As a young girl, Essie often heard her grandfather's harrowing account of how the Ku Klux Klan burned their house down and literally chased the Cardozo family from South Carolina when Reconstruction collapsed and the old order reigned supreme again.

Essie's father was a well-known educator, and her mother was a proud and dignified woman of regal bearing and aristocratic ways.

She gained quite a reputation in Washington for her independence. Almost every night, Mrs. Goode had to walk home from work through Washington's most desolate area—the cemetery. The worst crimes took place there, but no one ever bothered Mrs. Goode, because every Sunday afternoon she set up tin cans on her backyard fence, then shot them off the fence with her pistol, for all the neighbors to see and hear. So on her nightly walks, she strode confidently, with one hand in her purse.

In New York, Essie completed school and, college degree in hand, began a career as a lab technician at Columbia Presbyterian Hospital. She became the first Black analytical chemist there. In 1921, she met and married Paul, and seven years later she gave birth to their only child, my father, Paul, Jr. She was probably the single most influential person in launching and guiding my grandfather's career. For years, she handled much of his business—arranging contracts, travel itineraries, correspondence, and press relations and often pushing Paul to consider possibilities that might otherwise have been ignored.

(Opposite page) Eslanda Cardozo Goode Robeson (1896–1965), London, 1925. (Photo by Sasha/Courtesy of Paul Robeson, Jr.)

Paul's father, the Reverend William Drew Robeson
(1845–1918). (Courtesy of Paul Robeson, Jr.)

Paul's mother, Maria Louisa Bustill Robeson (1853–1904). (Courtesy of Paul Robeson, Jr.)

Paul's brother the Reverend Benjamin C. Robeson with the First Lady, Eleanor Roosevelt, at International Ministers Meeting, Salem Methodist Church, New York, March 19, 1945. (Courtesy of United Press International.)

With brother Ben, pastor of A.M.E. Zion Church, in church parsonage, Harlem, 1950s. (Courtesy of Paul Robeson, Jr.)

With Ben and their youngest sister, Marian Forsythe, in parsonage of A.M.E. Zion Church, Harlem, 1950s. (Photo by A. Hansen/Courtesy of Paul Robeson, Jr.)

My grandmother was a rather small woman, but possessed of boundless energy and a pioneer's spirit. Some found her pushy, others hard, and still others, charming. But above it all, she was brilliant and found herself at odds with society's definition of the proper place for a woman — much less a Black woman who was a scientist, anthropologist, journalist, and world traveler.

During the decade they lived in London, after Paul's opening in *Show Boat* in 1928, Essie became fascinated with anthropology — her interest was Africa and she began to study in some of England's most prestigious schools under the tutelage of men like Malinowski, one of the leading anthropologists of the era. Essie soon confronted the racism that permeated anthropology — a view of Africans as primitive and savage, incapable of achieving the heights of "civilization" in the European sense. Paul, at this time, was also deeply involved in explorations of African culture and languages, and he and Essie both found their way into the organizations and homes of the many Africans who worked or studied in London.

Essie decided this wasn't enough. Always ambitious, she took off for Africa in 1936, with young Paul, who was only eight. They began in South Africa and for several months traveled through Mozambique, Swaziland, Kenya, Uganda, and Egypt. Almost everywhere Essie went, Africans asked about Paul and were anxious for news of Black people in America. The trip was overwhelming and revelatory for both Essie and young Paul. Several years later, she published a book, *African Journey*, about the trip.

This trip always fascinated and impressed me. In the 1930s, a large percentage of Black Americans were ashamed of Africa and imagined the continent to be jungles filled with half-naked savages; most recoiled at the thought of an African heritage. My first impressions of Africa came from the stories of this trip my father would tell, my grandmother's accounts, and the numerous photos she took. To this day, I wear some of the jewelry that was given to her on that trip.

After returning from Africa, Essie went with Paul on his first trip to the Soviet Union and then accompanied him to Spain during the height of the Spanish Civil War.

The 1940s found Essie still involved in her anthropological studies, working toward her doctorate. She arranged the purchase of an estate in Enfield, Connecticut, which became their home for several years. They were forced to sell it in 1951 when Paul was under political attack, but Paul didn't mind, never having enjoyed its lavishness as Essie did. At Enfield, Essie pursued her literary interests, completing *African Journey*, and realized a longtime interest in photography, setting up a darkroom to process the hundreds of photos taken during the African trip.

Essie began to lecture, and developed a public stature apart from Paul. During her travels she met Pearl S. Buck. Essie's intellect and independence impressed Pearl Buck, and they became lasting friends. They lectured together on occasion and co-authored a book called *American Argument*, about the role of women in society. In 1949 Essie traveled to China, the guest of the new revolutionary government headed by Mao Zedong.

By the 1950s Essie was actively involved in the political movements that swirled around Paul. She was full of information, knew all kinds of people, and took great pride in keeping all the cross-currents interacting. Essie became a correspondent at the United Nations and spent much of the fifties observing world events through the insights of world leaders. She incessantly clipped articles and sent them with lengthy letters to friends and acquaintances all over the world. With this constant flow of communications, Essie was responsible for keeping Paul in touch with many important world figures and events around the world. In 1958, she traveled to Ghana for the great Accra Conference, the historic pan-African gathering of independence movements that brought African leaders together for the first time.

Throughout these years, when McCarthyism was at its height and Paul faced unrelenting persecution, Essie stood firmly at his side.

In 1953, she was called to testify before Joseph McCarthy himself, in televised hearings. She boldly stood her ground and even criticized the investigating committee for its inherent racism.

Essie died on the eve of her sixty-ninth birthday in 1965. She had been suffering from cancer for several years, but only the family and a few close friends had known. Essie had lived a unique and fulfilling life, as Mrs. Paul Robeson and in pursuing her own interests. She was a remarkable woman of fortitude and determination, with a tremendous capacity for work and an unbending dedication to the cause of freedom. Few women in her time traveled the world as she did, participated so fully in making history, or grew to such a heightened level of awareness of the world's problems.

Paul and Essie, Marseilles, France, 1936. (Courtesy of Paul Robeson, Jr.)

Paul and Eslanda, 1931. (Courtesy of Paul Robeson, Jr.)

Paul and Essie returning to New York after Paul's European concert tour, October 1935. (Courtesy of United Press International.)

Paul and Essie en route to Egypt to film *Jericho*, Marseilles, 1936. (Courtesy of Paul Robeson, Jr.)

Paul and Paul, Jr., age eight, England, 1936. (Courtesy of Paul Robeson, Jr.)

With young Paul, age eight, Plymouth, England, 1936. (Courtesy of United Press International.)

Paul, Jr., with Pygmy elder states-
men, Congo, 1936. (Photo by Eslanda
Robeson/Courtesy of Paul Robeson, Jr.)

Essie and young Paul, age two,
London, 1930. (Courtesy of Paul
Robeson, Jr.)

Paul, Jr., Essie's mother — Mama Goode — and Essie returning from London to settle in New York, 1939. (Photo by Morgan Smith.)

With Paul, Jr. a senior in Springfield Technical High School, at the Enfield, Connecticut, home, 1946.

Paul, Jr., showing the historic salute of Spanish Loyalists during Spanish Civil War, 1939. (Courtesy of Paul Robeson, Jr.)

107

(Opposite page) Essie *(standing left)* in Uganda during anthropological-research trip to Africa, 1936. (Courtesy of Paul Robeson, Jr.)

Softball game with cast of *Othello,* Central Park, New York, 1944. (Courtesy of Paul Robeson, Jr./Photo by Abraham Mandlestam.)

With Paul, Jr., and Clarence Muse, Enfield home, 1946.

Softball game with cast of *Othello,* Central Park, New York, 1944. (Courtesy of Paul Robeson, Jr./Photo by Abraham Mandlestam.)

Enfield, Connecticut, home, 1941. (Photo by Frank Bauman/Courtesy of Look Magazine.)

Enfield, Connecticut, home, 1941. (Photo by
Frank Bauman/Courtesy of Look Magazine.)

Enfield, Connecticut, home, 1941. (Photo by Frank Bauman/Courtesy of Look Magazine.)

111

Enfield, Connecticut, home, 1941. (Photo by Frank Bauman/Courtesy of Look Magazine.)

Enfield, Connecticut, home, 1941. (Photo by
Frank Bauman/Courtesy of Look Magazine.)

Essie, 1950. (Courtesy of *New York Daily News.*)

Backstage with dancer Paul Draper, New York, 1940s.
(Courtesy of Paul Robeson, Jr.)

Eslanda Robeson, Susan Robeson, and Paul Robeson at Russian circus, 1959. (Courtesy of Paul Robeson, Jr.)

My brother David Paul Robeson, baptism at A.M.E. Zion Church, 1952.

116

4
THE PINNACLE OF FAME AND FORTUNE

In the summer of 1939, with World War II smoldering in Europe, my grandparents decided to return to the United States to live. They had made London home base for more than a decade, ever since Paul's spectacular opening in *Show Boat* in 1928. They had made only brief trips to America for concert tours, but now Paul felt a responsibility to return home and immerse himself in the movements for change in America. He also wanted to take his proper place in the world of American theater and music.

Paul and Larry Brown had just completed a breathtaking but harrowing tour of Europe. Everywhere they went, Paul witnessed the tightening of Hitler's stranglehold on Europe. It was most intense in Norway, Denmark, and Sweden. The Scandinavian people turned out by the tens of thousands to hear Paul sing. He was a hero to them, and his concerts turned into huge anti-Nazi demonstrations. The message Paul carried in his music was so powerful that the Nazis banned his records.

Paul realized that he belonged at home with his people: "Having helped on many fronts, I feel that it is now time for me to return to the place of my origin—to those roots which,

though embedded in Negro life, are essentially American and are so regarded by the people of most other countries."[1]

In the fall of 1939, the Robeson family—Paul, Essie, and young Paul, now eleven—set sail for New York City. Two months later, Paul was in the studios of the Columbia Broadcasting System for the premiere broadcast of a new eleven-minute ballad by composer Earl Robinson. Six hundred people packed the studio for the momentous live broadcast of "Ballad for Americans":

Man in white skin can never be free
While his black brother is in slavery. . . .
Out of the cheating, out of the shouting,
Out of the windbags and patriotic spouting,
Out of uncertainty and doubting,
Out of the carpetbag and the brass spitoon,
It will come again—our marching song will come
  again,
Simple as a hit tune, deep as our valleys,
High as the mountains, strong as the people
  who made it.

As the broadcast ended, the radio audience could hear the beginning of the wild twenty-minute standing ovation from the studio audience. The CBS switchboard lit up with thousands of calls—it was the greatest audience response since Orson Welles's famous "Martian scare."

"Ballad for Americans" was immediately recorded, and within a year more than thirty thousand copies were sold. It became so popular that many considered it the unofficial national anthem. In 1940, the Republican party even selected "Ballad for Americans" as the theme song for the Republican National Convention. Paul was catapulted to new heights of fame.

Over the next few years, Paul and Larry toured the length and breadth of the United States several times. They performed everywhere, to overflow crowds: at the Hollywood Bowl, 30,000; Lewisohn Stadium in New York, where General de Gaulle of France joined Paul on the platform, 14,000; Grant Park in Chicago, 160,000; the Watergate in Washington, 22,000. Paul was one of the most popular concert artists in America and the most prominent Black man in the world.

My grandfather had matured artistically in the decade he spent abroad, and so had his social and political consciousness. Even with his success and wealth, he refused to let his own advancement obscure the degradation and racism that oppressed Black people—and he said so publicly, at every opportunity. He was the first major concert artist to refuse to perform before segregated audiences, and for this reason he turned down many lucrative offers to tour the Deep South. Southern promoters refused to honor the clause that became standard in all of Paul's contracts—a guarantee of no discrimination in seating or ticket sales.

Paul was the first major concert artist to perform inside prisons. And the entrance of Blacks into major-league baseball was also due, in part, to his efforts. In 1943, Paul led a delegation to meet with the commissioner of baseball, Kenesaw Mountain Landis, and the major-league club owners. He addressed them as a former athlete who, almost a quarter of a century earlier, had broken down racial barriers in college and professional football. Soon after this meeting, Jackie Robinson

was allowed to play for the Brooklyn Dodgers.

Nor had Paul forgotten colonized Africa in his newfound status and success in America. In 1937, he became one of the co-founders of the Council on African Affairs and shared the chairmanship with Dr. W. E. B. Du Bois. Over the years, Du Bois and Paul became close friends. Dr. Alpheous Hunton was another bedrock of the Council on African Affairs, and together he and Paul worked and studied to further African liberation, until the Council was forced to dissolve in 1955, owing to unrelenting government harassment. Hunton was jailed for his refusal to name names and inform on his co-workers. The Council stood alone in its earliest years, dedicated to African independence and to educating Black Americans about their historical and cultural roots in Africa. This was three decades before the cries of "Black power" and "Black is beautiful." The Council maintained official-observer status at the United Nations as well as contacts with all the liberation movements and revolutionary leaders in Africa. They counted such prominent Black artists as Lena Horne and Marian Anderson among their loyal supporters.

My grandfather's activism and world consciousness were mirrored and harmonized in his music. His repertoire expanded to include the folk music of other nationalities, songs of the anti-Nazi resistance movement, and songs from the labor movement in America. And always, Paul studied and sang songs in their original languages, to better communicate the subtleties of emotion and meaning. Critics across the country were virtually unanimous in proclaiming my grandfather one of the world's greatest interpretive artists.

Paul also found the time to immerse himself in the labor movement. "It seemed strange to some," he later commented, "that having attained some status and acclaim as an artist, I should devote so much time and energy to the problems and struggles of working men and women. To me, of course, it is not strange at all. I have simply tried never to forget the soil from which I spring."[2]

Paul walked scores of picket lines throughout the country and was awarded honorary memberships in several major unions, including the longshoremen's and maritime unions. He boldly supported the auto workers in Detroit in the 1940s, walking their picket lines when most were too frightened of the consequences. And Paul helped to build the CIO. At the heart of his labor activism was a burning desire to see Black and White workers unified, without which, Paul felt, union movements could easily be destroyed.

In 1941, America entered World War II. The nation now sought the goodwill of the Black community, and as a result some of the discrimination in government jobs slackened to include Black people in the war-production effort. Ironically, the military remained segregated while hundreds of thousands of Black men sacrificed their lives on foreign soil for the cause of freedom.

Paul joined in the war effort, along with many other prominent artists and celebrities, and he performed throughout the country and overseas for the government and the armed forces. Unbeknown to Paul, sinister forces in government, led by the FBI, had long since targeted him as dangerous; they considered his activism to be against the best interests of the American government. While Paul was touring the world and the nation on behalf of the American war effort, he was secretly placed on the "DetCom List." In case of a national emergency, Paul would be detained as a "communist" and jailed in a concentration camp with others similarly targeted. Ironically, at this moment my grandfather was being swept to the heights of national prominence and was looked to as an international hero and a role model by countless millions around the world.

"Ballad for Americans" radio broadcast, 1943. (Photo by Herbert Gehr/Courtesy of Life Pictures.)

I feel closer to my country than ever. There is no longer a feeling of lonesome isolation. Instead —peace. I return without fearing prejudice that once bothered me . . . for I know that people practice cruel bigotry in their ignorance, not maliciously. . . .

I've learned that my people are not the only ones oppressed. . . . I have sung my songs all over the world and everywhere found that some common bond makes the people of all lands take to Negro songs as their own.

When I sang my American folk melodies in Budapest, Prague, Tiflis, Moscow, Oslo, or the Hebrides or on the Spanish front, the people understood and wept or rejoiced with the spirit of the songs. I found that where forces have been the same, whether people weave, build, pick cotton, or dig in the mine, they understand each other in the common language of work, suffering, and protest.[3]

New York Interview
1939

Live premiere broadcast of "Ballad for Americans," conducted by André Kostelanetz, CBS radio studio, New York, 1939. (Courtesy of Paul Robeson, Jr.)

It means so little when a man like me wins some success. Where is the benefit when a small class of Negroes makes money and can live well? It may all be encouraging, but it has no deeper significance.

I feel this way because I have cousins who can neither read nor write. I have had a chance. They have not. That is the difference.[4]

Wisconsin Interview
1941

San Quentin Prison, California, 1941. (Courtesy of Taylor Davis Collection.)

Radio broadcast with Raymond Massey, New York, 1943. (Courtesy of Paul Robeson, Jr.)

With Carl Van Vechten at dinner party honoring Marian Anderson, New York, 1939. (Photo by Albert Fenn/Life Pictures.)

Recording "King Joe," a tribute to Joe Louis, with Count Basie and his orchestra, New York, 1942. (Photo by Eliot Elisofon/Life Pictures.)

(*Opposite page*) At a children's camp, 1941. (Courtesy of Paul Robeson, Jr.)

The Savoy Ballroom, Harlem, 1941. (Photo by Morgan Smith.)

New York, 1942. (Courtesy of Paul Robeson, Jr.)

The talents of an artist, small or great, are God given. They've nothing to do with him as a private person; they're nothing to be proud of. They're just a sacred trust. . . .

Having been given, I must give. Man shall not live by bread alone, and what the farmer does I must do. I must feed the people—with my songs.[5]

London Interview
1930

At the A.M.E. Zion Church, Harlem, 1941. (Courtesy of Morgan Smith.)

Bennett College, Greensboro, North Carolina, 1942.
(Courtesy of Paul Robeson, Jr.)

I had never put a correct evaluation on the dignity and courage of my people of the Deep South until I began to come South myself. . . . Deep down, I think I had imagined Negroes of the South beaten, subservient, cowed. But I see them now courageous and possessors of a profound and instinctive dignity, a race that has gone through its trials unbroken, a race of such magnificence of spirit that there exists no power on earth that could crush them. They will bend, but they will never break. . . .

I have traveled extensively. I have seen people in all parts of the world: peoples who, some of them, have not been equal to the spiritual task of retaining dignity and self-respect and courage and self-reli-ance. I have seen whole peoples ground down, depleted, crushed. But not so these great Black people. Nothing the future brings can defeat a people who have come through three hundred years of slavery and humiliation and privation with heads high and eyes clear and straight. . . .

We must come south to understand in their starkest presentation the common problems that beset us everywhere. We must breathe the smoke of battle. We must taste the bitterness, see the ugli-ness. . . . We must expose ourselves un-remittingly to the source of strength that makes the black South strong![6]

New Orleans Speech
1942

127

Concert in Chicago, 1945

After meeting with Baseball Commissioner Landis and major league owners, pressuring for end to discrimination in major leagues, December 3, 1943. (Courtesy of Paul Robeson, Jr.)

Workers' concert on Oakland docks, September 20, 1942. (Courtesy of *Daily World.*)

With Congressman Adam Clayton Powell, Jr., and Malcolm Ross, Chairman of the Fair Employment Practices Committee Campaign, during third annual Negro Freedom Rally, Madison Square Garden, June 25, 1945. (Courtesy of UPI.)

Council on African Affairs meeting, New York, 1947. (*Left to right, rear,* Louis Burnham, Charles Collins, Maude Clark, and Alphaeus Hunton.) (Courtesy of Paul Robeson, Jr.)

With Marian Anderson at Council on African Affairs campaign for South African Famine Relief, Abyssinian Baptist Church, Harlem, 1946. (Courtesy of Photo World.)

130

With Indian student leaders at Council on African Affairs symposium, "Africa in the War and World Peace," International House, New York, 1941. (Photo by Morgan Smith.)

"Stars for China," War-relief benefit, Philadelphia, May 2, 1941. (Courtesy of Paul Robeson, Jr.)

Concert for naval workers, 1942. (Courtesy of Paul Robeson, Jr.)

With officials of Future Outlook League, Cleveland, 1945. (Courtesy of Paul Robeson, Jr.)

If America is to survive in this new world, she will have to deal with millions of Negroes who will no longer be in bondage.[7]

War-bond rally, Pittsburgh, 1945. (Courtesy of Paul Robeson, Jr.)

Leaving for Europe on first integrated USO overseas tour of performing artists for U.S. troops, August 1945. (Courtesy of Paul Robeson, Jr.)

With Lena Horne, war-bond campaign, 1942. (Courtesy of Paul Robeson, Jr.)

With actress Gertrude Lawrence, war-relief benefit, Dennis, Massachusetts, 1942. (Courtesy of Paul Robeson, Jr.)

With the first lady, Eleanor Roosevelt, at "Salute to Negro Troops," Cosmopolitan Opera House, January 12, 1942. (Courtesy of UPI.)

With Vice-President Henry Wallace, 1943. (Courtesy of Paul Robeson, Jr./Photo by Rus Arnold.)

With Nigerian President Namide Azikiwe and Essie at third-anniversary celebration of Nigerian independence, United Nations, 1963. (Courtesy of *Freedomways*.)

Relaxing at resort near Yalta with Soviet Premier Nikita
Khrushchev, Crimea, 1958. (Courtesy of Paul Robeson, Jr.)

With Prime Minister Jawaharlal
Nehru of India, New York, 1957.
(Courtesy of Paul Robeson, Jr.)

With writers Carl Sandburg and Jan Struther, about 1940. (Courtesy of Paul Robeson, Jr.)

With Leontyne Price at joint concert, Dayton, Ohio, 1940s. (Courtesy of Paul Robeson, Jr.)

With Marian Anderson during dinner
in her honor, New York, 1939.
(Photo by Morgan Smith.)

With composer W. C. Handy at Paul's forty-sixth birthday celebration, New York Armory, 1944. (Courtesy of *Daily World.*)

Addressing luncheon in honor of Lillian Hellman, New York, December 1944. (*Left to right,* Herman Shumlin, Moss Hart, Paul, Margaret Webster, Raymond Massey, Lillian Hellman.) (Courtesy of *The Guardian.*)

Donaldson Awards: Paul is given award for Best Male Performance in Play for 1944. New York, July 3, 1944.

With Cab Calloway and Richard Wright at opening of *Native Son*, March 13, 1941. (Photo by Morgan Smith.)

American Academy of Arts and Letters, Paul awarded Medal for Good Diction on the Stage. Standing, left to right, Samuel S. McClure, Willa Cather, Theodore Dreiser. New York, May 19, 1944.

With Hal Johnson, Josh White, Ethel Waters, and Canada Lee, 1944. (Courtesy of Paul Robeson, Jr.)

With Joe Louis at his training camp, 1946. (Courtesy of *Photo World.*)

With Leadbelly, Sonny Terry, and Cisco Houston, benefit for National Negro Congress, New York, September 4, 1946. (Courtesy of *Daily World.*)

The *Othello* production of 1942-45 was my grandfather's crowning achievement as an actor. Paul's interpretation and performance revolutionized Shakespearean theater in modern times. His *Othello* was hailed as a classic and stands today as the yardstick for measuring the greatness of others, including such eminent actors as Laurence Olivier and Orson Welles, in portraying Othello.

Paul ruffled many in the theatrical world of England when he first performed *Othello* there in 1930. Almost seventy years had passed since a Black man—the great Ira Aldridge—had played Othello onstage. With the exception of Aldridge, Othello was played in modern times by White men carefully darkened to appear more Arab than African . . . until Paul. My grandfather drew on the traditions of history that the world had forgotten or hidden. He thoroughly researched the matter and discovered that before Edmund Kean, the greatest Shakespearean actor of the eighteenth century, Othello had always been played by Black men, based on Shakespeare's conception of the character. Shakespeare's own leading actor, Richard Burbage, played Othello as a Black man. The onslaught of slavery in the eighteenth century and the subsequent domination of Africa changed all that. Paul wrote in the early 1940s,

Shakespeare meant Othello to be a Black Moor from Africa, an African of the highest nobility of heritage. From Kean on, Othello was made a light-skinned Moor because western Europe had made Africa a slave center, and the African was pictured as a slave. English critics seeing a Black Othello—like my Othello—were likely to take a colonial point of view and regard him off-hand as low and ignoble. . . .

Shakespeare's play has deep social meaning today. Shakespeare saw his era in human terms, an era of change from the feudal to higher forms of social relationships. In Othello, he anticipated the rape of Africa and some of the subsequent racial problems.[8]

Paul's ideas were shocking to Americans in the 1940s. Margaret Webster, the eventual producer, later commented, "There was so much fear in the public's race prejudice that

producers were skeptical about putting money into it. Everybody was scared. Most of them said an American audience would never come to a theater to see a Black man play a love scene with a white woman. I believed that a production of the play with [Robeson] in it could be a landmark in American theater and in the history of American social consciousness."[9] A superb cast was assembled, with Uta Hagen as Desdemona and José Ferrer playing Iago.

Othello first opened at the Brattle Hall Theatre in Cambridge, Massachusetts, during the summer of 1942. It met with critical acclaim and then traveled to Princeton, New Haven, Boston, and Philadelphia. But everyone was awaiting the New York opening on Broadway. *Variety* described the upcoming event as one that would "hurl Broadway on its practically invulnerable ear."

In the fall of 1943, *Othello* opened at the Shubert Theatre on Broadway. New York critics praised the production and hailed Paul's performance:

"Unquestionably the finest portrayal of Shakespeare's tragic Moor to be given in this generation."[10]

"Othello is so illuminated and held in a taut and thrilling pattern that it becomes in many respects, something new and wonderful in the theatre."[11]

"Paul Robeson gives the outstanding performance in New York."[12]

"One of the most memorable events in the history of the theatre. . . . There has never been and never will be a finer rendition of this particular tragedy. It is unbelievably magnificent. . . . There has simply been nothing on Broadway in years to earn our gratitude to the theatre more profoundly."[13]

Othello broke all Broadway records for Shakespearean productions, with a record run of 296 consecutive performances, by far surpassing the previous record of 157 performances set by Orson Welles's production of *Julius Caesar*.

After almost ten months on Broadway, *Othello* toured the United States and Canada—going everywhere except the South. My grandfather refused to perform there because

142

(Opposite page) Othello, Shubert Theatre, New York, 1943. (Photo by Ellie Marcus/Courtesy of Paul Robeson, Jr.)

Othello has killed Desdemona. From savage passion? No.

Othello came from a culture as great as that of ancient Venice. He came from an Africa of equal stature. And he felt he was betrayed. He felt his honor was betrayed and his human dignity was betrayed.[14]

143

of segregated audiences. When *Othello* finally closed in 1945, more than half a million people had seen it. Paul was graced with many honors, but two stand out. The American Academy of Arts and Letters awarded him the Medal for Good Diction on the Stage in 1944. Only nine people have ever received that award since its inception in the 1920s. He was also given the First Annual Donaldson Award—the equivalent of today's Tony—for Outstanding Lead Performance of 1944.

Part of Paul's success and the production's unique quality was that it brought Shakespeare to a mass audience that ranged from the White cultural elite to all echelons of the Black community and working people. Those who ordinarily found Shakespeare alien discovered *Othello* to be an exciting and meaningful experience. Paul viewed his triumph as more than an artistic success. To him it was a social weapon. Paul was catapulted to the heights of national stardom and hailed as "America's number-one Negro" and a role model for America's youth.

Othello, with Uta Hagen as Desdemona, Shubert Theatre, New York, 1942. (Photo by George Karger/Life Pictures.)

(Opposite page) Othello, with José Ferrer as Iago, Shubert Theatre, New York, 1943. (Photo by George Karger/Life Pictures.)

Othello confronting José Ferrer, as Iago, Shubert Theatre, New York, 1943. (Photo Herbert Gehr/Life Pictures)

(Opposite page) Othello, with Uta Hagen as Desdemona, Shubert Theatre, New York, 1942. (Photo by George Karger/Life Pictures.)

Othello, with Uta Hagen as Desdemona, 1943. (Photo by Herbert Gehr/Life Pictures.)

Othello, with Uta Hagen as Desdemona, 1943. (Courtesy
of Vandam Pictures/Paul Robeson, Jr.)

149

It was deeply fascinating to watch how strikingly contemporary American audiences from coast to coast found Shakespeare's Othello *painfully immediate in its unfolding of evil, innocence, passion, dignity, and nobility and contemporary in its overtones of a clash of cultures, of the partial acceptance of, and consequent effect upon, one of a minority group. Against this background the jealousy of the protagonist becomes more credible, the blows to his pride more understandable, the final collapse of his personal, individual world more inevitable. But beyond the personal tragedy, the terrible agony of Othello, the irretrievability of his world, the complete destruction of all trusted and sacred values —all these suggest the shattering of a universe. . . .*

Now, interestingly enough, we stand at the end of one period in human history and before the entrance of a new. All our tenets and tried beliefs are challenged.[15]

150

Madison Square Garden, New York, 1947. (Photo by Bernard Cole/Courtesy of Paul Robeson, Jr.)

5
THE POLITICS OF PERSECUTION

The death of President Roosevelt in 1945 brought Missouri's Harry Truman into office. Truman beat a fast retreat from the radical social and economic policies of Roosevelt's New Deal. The tenor of the times began to change, setting the stage for the conservatism of an approaching Cold War era. World War II was over. Black soldiers were returning home. Having fought overseas to preserve democracy, they expected to find it back home. Instead, a wave of brutal lynchings and beatings swept the country, particularly in the South. Ironically, at this moment Paul stood at the pinnacle of fame, fortune, and success in America. He had the whole world in his hands.

Paul and Larry set out on concert tours across the country in 1946 and 1947. Never had Paul done so many concerts or been received with such warmth. My grandfather was deeply affected by the contradiction of his personal success at a time when Black people faced increasing hardship. Larry Brown later reflected, "It's irony that at the peak of his career, and at the moment when I think he reached his zenith, he was more difficult to work with than during all the years before. He was in a terrible mood. He constantly felt he could not sing another concert."[1]

In the fall of 1946, Paul led a delegation to Washington, D.C., as part of the Anti-Lynching Crusade and sought a personal audience with President Truman. Paul was invited to the White House, where he met privately with the president. It was a stormy meeting. My grandfather had come to demand, in no uncertain terms, that Truman use his presidential powers to ensure the protection of Black people in the South from the lynchings that were taking place with alarming regularity.

When my grandfather emerged from the meeting, he was surrounded by a large crowd of reporters. After a barrage of hostile questions, he was finally asked, "Are you a communist?"

"I label myself violently antifascist," Paul responded.

Another reporter asked if he believed in "turning the other cheek."

"If someone hit me on one cheek," Paul retorted, "I'd tear his head off before he could hit me on the other one."

America was severely traumatized. The press was now openly hostile toward Paul, and the forces of reaction began to circle.

Less than one month after Paul's White House meeting he was subpoenaed by the California Legislative Committee on Un-

American Activities, known as the Tenney Committee. The original purpose of the Tenney Committee was to investigate incidents of Ku Klux Klan cross burnings in California, but instead the hearings were used as a pretext to harass and intimidate progressive people. My grandfather was one of those targeted. The Tenney Committee questioned him vociferously about his political ideas and associations. They were determined to label him a communist and therefore against the best interests of the American people. The committee seemed to have forgotten that only a few years before, during World War II, communists were among America's most determined allies and considered among the most heroic resistance fighters against fascism. But fascism was no longer the enemy. To the forces of reaction, communism was the number-one threat in the world.

My grandfather stated before the Tenney Committee that he was not and had never been a member of the Communist party. But as the proceedings continued, he refused to acknowledge the committee's distorted view of communism as an enemy of the American people. His experience and understanding of world events had taught him that fascism was most to be feared. But this did not interest the Tenney Committee. The committee became the tool for those who wanted to shut Paul up or make him pay a price for his outspoken ideas.

Paul continued his concert tours with great success, though a few were canceled by local promoters. In March 1947, several months after the Tenney Committee hearings, he arrived in Salt Lake City for one of the last concerts of his 1947 tour. Twenty years earlier, a now famous union organizer, Joe Hill, had met his death there by execution in Utah's state prison. Salt Lake City was the copper bosses' town then, and Joe Hill became a martyr to the labor movement. Paul closed his concert with a ballad immortalizing Joe Hill. It had never been sung before in Salt Lake City, and it stunned the audience with its militant memorialization of Joe Hill.

Then Paul made an announcement.

"You've heard my final concert for at least two years, and perhaps for many more. I'm retiring here and now from concert work—I shall sing, from now on, for my trade-union and college friends; in other words, only at gatherings where I can sing what I please."[2]

The audience was shocked. Here was a man who had reached his zenith. He was rich and famous by all standards and yet willing to sacrifice it all for his principles. Meanwhile, Congressman J. Parnell Thomas, chairman of the House Un-American Activities Committee (HUAC), was taking testimony in the nation's capital to discredit my grandfather and prove that he was a communist.

In April, the final legs of Paul's 1947 tour took him to southern Illinois, a bastion of conservatism and bigotry. He was scheduled to sing in Peoria, but by the time he arrived the concert had been canceled and the mayor had called the City Council into special session. The mayor demanded that the City Council pass a special ordinance barring my grandfather from Peoria. The legal justification was a law giving the mayor power "to take steps necessary to prevent riots and other disturbances."

Paul was labeled an "avowed or active propagandist for un-American ideologies." Fourteen armed policemen were dispatched to the train station to prevent him from entering Peoria. This was the first organized attempt to deny the public the right to hear my grandfather sing. The press baited Paul, as was becoming their style, but his message was simple: "Since when in America does a city dare keep an artist out because of his political opinions?"

Two weeks later, Paul was scheduled to give a concert in Albany, New York—the last of his tour. The mayor there forced the Board of Education to withdraw permission for a school auditorium to be used for the concert as scheduled. The concert's sponsors initiated legal action, and after two weeks of battling in the courts the concert was held under a judge's order.

The following month, June 1947, Paul left for Panama for a series of concerts sponsored by the United Public Workers of the CIO, who were working to unionize predominantly Black Panamanian workers. The most successful concert was to a crowd of ten thousand in Panama City with the president of Panama, don Enrique Jiménez, in attendance.

Then Paul flew to Hawaii, where he gave fifteen concerts.

In 1948, Paul made his first and only trip to the Caribbean. He toured Trinidad and then Jamaica, where the people turned out by the thousands, welcoming him as a national hero. His concert in Jamaica was attended by more than twenty thousand people and is still remembered as a momentous occasion. Norman Manley, prime minister of Jamaica from 1959-62, and his son Michael Manley, prime minister of Jamaica from 1972-80, extended a warm welcome to my grandfather. He, in turn, was deeply moved by his experiences in Jamaica. This was his first trip to an independent Black nation, and it had a profound psychological impact on him as a Black man.

Meanwhile, a legislative bill known as the Mundt-Nixon Communist Control Bill was making its way through Congress. Many at the time considered it a thought-control bill that would effectively outlaw all opposition to the government, especially open criticism of American foreign policy. By June 1948, the bill was up for Senate hearings, and my grandfather was called to testify. By this time, HUAC was in continuous session, and the Hollywood Ten were on their way to jail for refusing to cooperate when called to testify.

Paul locked horns with the hostile investigating committee. When they finally asked him directly if he was a communist, Paul refused to answer, with full knowledge that he could be slapped with a jail sentence for contempt. But it was now a matter of principle for my grandfather. Years later, in describing why, Paul said, "Because by that time the Hollywood writers had gone to jail, and a great wave of anti-communist hysteria had set in. To answer such questions would have meant that I was contributing to the hysteria. So as a matter of principle I felt I had to invoke my constitutional right to say that my political

beliefs are nobody's business."[3] My grandfather was now on a collision course with the powers-that-be of America.

Earlier that year, in the spring of 1948, a major third political party, the Progressive party, had been formed to challenge the Democrats and Republicans in the upcoming presidential election. My grandfather was one of the founding members along with Henry Wallace, who was the vice-president under President Roosevelt and then a member of Harry Truman's cabinet. It was the first time in America's history that a Black person played a key role in the formation and political platform of a major political party.

During the summer and fall of 1948, Paul crisscrossed the country campaigning for Henry Wallace, the Progressive party's candidate for president. Everywhere he went, my grandfather received a tumultuous welcome, as though he were the presidential candidate. Soon the press began openly red-baiting the Progressive party, and when the campaign finally went South, they were met with violence. This was the most dangerous trip of my grandfather's entire life. He survived death threats from the Ku Klux Klan, and meetings were sometimes held under armed guard. Paul was never more outspoken. He lashed out at the manipulation of American popular opinion, which was heightening as the cold war heightened, and warned of the dangers of fascism in America. He pointed to the Klan, with their rising popularity, as the "cousins, if not the brothers, of Nazis in Germany."

As 1948 ended, eighty-five of my grandfather's concerts were canceled for the 1949 season. He faced a virtual American boycott. The intent was to force Paul to remain silent about his political opinions or sacrifice his career. My grandfather fought back, rather than retreat. "I decided to go to Europe to resume my professional concerts. I wanted to make it perfectly clear that the world is wide and a few pressures could not stop my career."[4]

Paul and Essie set sail for London in February 1949. Paul's reception was enthusiastic. Concerts in London and throughout the English provinces were an incredible success.

American Crusade to End Lynching rally, after White House meeting with President Truman, Lincoln Memorial, Washington, D.C., September 24, 1946. (Courtesy of UPI.)

ROBESON TELLS TRUMAN: DO SOMETHING ABOUT LYNCHINGS OR NEGROES WILL

Washington—Paul Robeson, Negro baritone, spearhead of the American Crusade to End Lynching, said yesterday after a White House visit that he had told the President that if the Government did not do something to curb lynching, "Negroes would."

To this statement, Robeson said, the President took sharp exception. The President, he said, remarked that it sounded like a threat. Robeson told newspapermen he assured the President it was not a threat but merely a statement of fact about the temper of the Negro people. . . .

Robeson asked the President to make a formal declaration of disapproval of lynching within the next 100 days. Robeson explained the next 100 days would be an appropriate time for the President to act, because it was on September 22, 1862, that Lincoln issued the proclamation freeing the slaves and it was on January 1st that it became effective.

The President, Robeson said, told the delegation that Government action against lynching was necessarily a political matter, and that timing was important. The President, Robeson reported, said that this was not the time for him to act.

The singer said he also pointed out what he considered misdirections in American foreign policy. He said it was hard to see the distinction between current lynchings and the Nuremburg war crimes trials. He explained that he meant by this that the United States could not logically take the lead in punishing the Nazis for the oppression of groups in Germany while the Government here permitted Negroes to be lynched and shot. To this, he said, the President objected that loyal Americans should not mix domestic problems like lynching with foreign policy. Robeson said he told the President he did not see how the two could be separated.[5]

157

After press conference in Peoria, Illinois, where the city banned a Robeson concert, April 1947. (Courtesy of AP.)

Council on African Affairs Rally for South African Famine Relief, Abyssinian Baptist Church, Harlem, January 7, 1946. (Courtesy of *Photo World.*)

Concert held under court order, Larry Brown accompanying. Livingston Junior High School, Albany, New York, May 11, 1947. (Courtesy of UPI.)

With president of Panama, Enrique Jiménez, and Larry Brown after open-air concert in Panama City, June 1947. (Courtesy of Paul Robeson, Jr.)

With Benjamin J. Davis, Jr., longtime friend and city councilman from Harlem, May Day celebration, Union Square, New York, 1947. (Courtesy of UPI.)

QUESTION: *Are you an American Communist?*

ROBESON: *. . . Some of the most brilliant and distinguished Americans are about to go to jail for failure to answer that question and I am going to join them, if necessary. I refuse to answer the question.*[6]

Testimony before Senate Committee
Hearings on Mundt-Nixon Bill, June 1948

Testifying at U.S. Senate hearings on Mundt-Nixon Bill,
Washington, D.C., June 1948. (Courtesy of Paul Robeson,
Jr.)

Progressive party nominating convention, Philadelphia, June 1948. (Photo by Julius Lazarus.)

Progressive party nominating convention, Philadelphia, June 1948. (Photo by Julius Lazarus.)

161

Progressive-party leaders, Philadelphia, July 1948. Seated to Paul's right are presidential candidate Henry Wallace and vice-presidential candidate Senator Glen Taylor. Behind Taylor is party chairman Rexford Tugwell. (Courtesy of UPI.)

Civil Rights Congress picketing at White House, August 1948. (Photo by Julius Lazarus.)

Progressive party campaign, Wallace for president, Madison Square Garden, 1948. (Courtesy of Tony Schwartz.)

With Vito Marcantonio, New York congressman, Progressive party presidential campaign, Yankee Stadium, New York, July 1948. (Photo by Julius Lazarus.)

With Lena Horne and presidential candidate Henry Wallace, 1948. (Photo by Llewellyn Ransom/Courtesy of Paul Robeson, Jr.)

163

The years of absence had only increased Paul's popularity. London was typical—ten thousand tickets went on sale one morning, and by noon they were completely sold out. And there were scores of meetings and huge rallies at which Paul spoke out against the saber rattling of American foreign policy and the misguided cold-war premises that made a false bogeyman of communism.

In April 1949, Paul flew to Paris to attend the World Peace Congress with seventeen thousand delegates from all over the world. The insignia of the conference was the white dove of peace—designed and painted by Pablo Picasso for the occasion. When Paul arrived, he was asked to address the conference on behalf of the thousands of Third World delegates. They wanted him to express their aspirations for independence from colonialism and, above all, for world peace. My grandfather made a short impromptu speech. It turned out to be the most controversial speech of his entire career . . . and the pretext for unleashing a decade of unprecedented persecution against him.

Paul talked about the contributions that colonial peoples have made to building the wealth of the world's industrial powers and their desire to share this wealth more equitably. He expressed their strong desire for world peace but a willingness to fight to maintain it, if necessary. And finally, he said, "It is unthinkable that American Negroes could go to war on behalf of those who have oppressed us for generations, against the Soviet Union, which in one generation has raised our people to full human dignity."[7] He touched America's Achilles' heel—the hypocrisy of claiming to be the leader of the "free world" while denying fundamental rights and freedoms to Black citizens.

American pressmen in Paris cabled my grandfather's statements back to the State Department, where they exploded like a bombshell. Paul was doing the unpardonable. He was mixing America's domestic problems with foreign policy; and he was a Black man criticizing the government's foreign policy before the world. This was unheard of and could not be tolerated. A systematic campaign was launched to discredit Paul and silence him.

Almost two weeks after my grandfather's speech in Paris, the American press began running glaring headlines distorting his statements and labeling them treason. Numerous editorials appeared all across the country denouncing Paul. The House Un-American Activities Committee was in session in Washington, and witnesses were subpoenaed to testify that Paul did not speak for Black Americans. A few Black leaders spoke up in support, but against tremendous pressure. The *Afro-American* newspaper carried an editorial that expressed the sentiments of many in the Black community. "Robeson said that he would much rather fight the southern whites who are denying equal rights to colored people than the Russians who have not done anything to us at all. . . . There have always been conscientious objectors and there are millions of colored Americans, too, who believe that Ku Kluxers and the bigots among the white race in the South are far more dangerous to them than the Russians."[8]

Meanwhile, my grandfather had flown to Norway from Paris for a series of concerts and then to Denmark, Poland, Czechoslovakia, and the Soviet Union for the remainder of his scheduled tour. In June, Paul and Essie came back to New York.

Paul knew he was returning home to face bitter attack. He had given it deep thought and resolved to stand firm. So grave did the consequences appear, that he prepared himself to accept the eventuality of even death— the atmosphere was that ominous. A host of uniformed police and a horde of reporters were at the airport for my grandfather's arrival. The reporters launched right into Paul— needling him about his Paris speech, saying that he was un-American, and baiting him about communism. But my grandfather reserved comment, telling the press to come to Harlem that weekend for his answers at the huge welcome-home rally being organized for him at Rockland Palace.

Paul had other things on his mind as well. Paul, Jr.—my father—had decided to marry.

He and my mother, Marilyn Paula Greenberg, had met a few years before at Cornell University, where they both attended school. The family realized there would be an intense public reaction, especially now. Interracial marriages were quite scandalous . . . and on top of that, it was Paul Robeson's son marrying a white woman. The press sensationalized the announcement and did everything they could to inflame the public mind and whip up hysteria.

My mother and father were married in the Manhattan home of a friend and minister. It was a private family affair with my mother's mother, Rae Greenberg, and her brother Harold in attendance. The press was barred completely, but every news editor in town had a reporter outside the wedding. A crowd of several hundred Whites also gathered. When the family emerged they were greeted by an angry White mob shouting racial epithets and were surrounded by a swarm of reporters snapping pictures and firing questions. Paul was livid with anger as he climbed into a waiting car with the others. Before they could drive off, a reporter stuck both his head and camera through the car window to take a picture. Paul exploded, incensed by such a crude invasion of privacy, and leaned forward to smash the camera and reporter in one swift motion. "I have the greatest contempt for the press. Only something within me keeps me from smashing your cameras over your heads."

That evening, my grandfather spoke at the welcome-home rally in Harlem. More than four thousand people attended. In the following months he continued to speak out on the most controversial issues of the day. Eleven Communist party members were on trial in New York for an alleged conspiracy to overthrow the government by force and violence. Paul spoke out in their defense. They were being tried for their political opinions, and Paul felt that if they were convicted, no one would be safe whose opinions opposed government policy.

The press distorted Paul's statements with scandalous headlines. Subtle threats against him began to appear in articles and editorials. The forces of reaction circled closer.

The hysteria that surrounded my parents'

With Larry Brown, accompanist, on eve of departure for European concert tour, Harlem, February 1949. (Courtesy of Julius Lazarus.)

In Oslo, Norway, during European concert tour, 1949. (Courtesy of Paul Robeson, Jr.)

Celebrating the birthday of Alexander Pushkin, the great Russian author of African descent, Moscow, 1949. (Courtesy of Paul Robeson, Jr.)

166

In concert, Warsaw, Poland, 1949.
(Courtesy of Paul Robeson, Jr.)

In concert, Moscow, 1949. (Courtesy of Paul Robeson, Jr.)

In concert, Prague, Czechoslovakia,
1949. (Courtesy of Paul Robeson, Jr.)

167

With workers and union leaders, Poland, 1949. (Courtesy of Paul Robeson, Jr.)

With Dr. W. E. B. DuBois, Paris Peace Conference, April 20, 1949. (Courtesy of UPI.)

We colonial peoples have contributed to the building of the United States and are determined to share in its wealth. We denounce the policy of the United States government which is similar to that of Hitler and Goebbels. We want peace and liberty and will combat for them along with the Soviet Union, the democracies of eastern Europe, China and Indonesia . . .

It is unthinkable that American Negroes could go to war on behalf of those who have oppressed us for generations against the Soviet Union which in one generation has raised our people to full human dignity.[9]

Speech at Paris Peace Conference
April 21, 1949

Delivering most controversial speech of his career, Paris Peace Conference, April 20, 1949. (Courtesy of Paul Robeson, Jr.)

Arrival at La Guardia after European tour and Paris Peace Conference, June 19, 1949. (Courtesy of *Daily News*.)

Motorcade from airport with Paul, Jr., June 1949. (Courtesy of Paul Robeson, Jr.)

170

My mother and father, Paul, Jr., and Marilyn Paula Greenberg, leaving private home where they married, New York, June 19, 1949. (Courtesy of *Daily News*.)

marriage was something I was aware of from early in my childhood. It fit together with everything else I was learning about my grandfather: The reactionary climate in America placed him at odds with the American establishment. By the late 1940s, everything he did in the political arena was controversial.

The older I got, the more enraged I became by the racism of the White reaction to my parents' marriage. Being extremely inquisitive, I read all the newsclippings, with their hysterical headlines, that my grandmother had carefully saved. They were always a reminder for me of the sick inability of White America to cope with human realities in human terms. All this served to make me a fighter before my time, because I realized that ultimately, my right to exist was being denied, that according to the prevailing standards in America I was inferior and an insult to White sensibilities.

As I learned my family history, the reaction to my parents' marriage in June of 1949 was always tied to the bitter public reaction to my grandfather's statements at the Paris Peace Conference two months earlier. Paris turned out to be another critical turning point in my grandfather's life. At the time it seemed rather inconsequential, but a few weeks after the Paris conference, the vicious reaction of the American government began to unfold. International press coverage of his speech at the time was not earthshattering, though coverage in the European press was extensive.

American reporters stationed in Europe routinely cabled their stories to both their editors and the State Department. Two weeks later, what now appears to have been an orchestrated reaction was unleashed. All the stories in the press about Robeson in Paris had a common theme: His comments in Paris were un-American, treasonous, and a threat to world peace, and further, he did not represent the sentiments of the Black community.

It seems that forces within the State Department determined that they could use my grandfather's statements in Paris as a pretext for launching a vicious campaign to discredit him and destroy his image. The rest is history.

My mother's mother, Rae Greenberg; Paul; and my mother's brother, Harold, leaving my parents' wedding, June 19, 1949. (A photographer is attempting to take another photo without permission.) UPI.

Today I defy any part of an insolent, dominating America, however powerful; I defy any errand boys, Uncle Toms of the Negro people, to challenge my Americanism, because by my word and deed I challenge this vicious system to the death because I refuse to let my personal success, as part of a fraction of one percent of the Negro people, explain away the injustices to fourteen million of my people. . . . I'm looking for freedom, full freedom, not an inferior brand. . . .

I am born and bred in this America of ours. I want to love it. I love a part of it. But it's up to the rest of America when I shall love it with the same intensity that I love the Negro people from whom I spring. . . .

The so-called western democracies — including our own . . . can find no answer before the bar of world justice for their treatment of the Negro people. . . . We must have the courage to shout at the top of our voices about our injustices and we must lay the blame . . . where it has belonged for over 300 years of slavery and misery, right here on our own doorstep — not in any faraway place. . . . We do not want to die in vain any more on foreign battlefields for Wall Street and the greedy supporters of domestic fascism. If we must die, let it be in Mississippi or Georgia! Let it be wherever we are lynched and deprived of our rights as human beings![10]

Speech at Welcome Home Rally
Rockland Palace
June 19, 1949

With members of Black press before a welcome-home rally for Paul, New York, June 1949. (Courtesy of *Daily World*.)

Welcome-home rally at Rockland Palace, Harlem, June
19, 1949. (Courtesy of Ira Rosenberg/Paul Robeson, Jr.)

173

Civil Rights Congress rally, Washington, D.C., June 1949. (Courtesy of Julius Lazarus.)

Madison Square Garden, New York, 1949. (Photo by Julius Lazarus/Courtesy of Paul Robeson, Jr.)

I am a radical and I am going to stay one until my people get free to walk the earth. Negroes just cannot wait for civil rights. [11]

With Bessie Mitchell, sister of Trenton Six defendant, and William Patterson, chairman of the Civil Rights Congress. (Courtesy of *Daily World*.)

Picketing the White House in protest of discriminatory employment practices, August 4, 1949. (Louis Burnham, editor of *Freedom* magazine, in foreground.) (Courtesy of UPI.)

Entrance to concert grounds at Peekskill, New York, September 4, 1949. (Courtesy of United Press International.)

Since the summer of 1946, Peekskill had been the site of an annual open-air concert by Paul Robeson. It was always an all-day family affair with tens of thousands of people coming by bus and car from New York City and the surrounding area in upstate New York. The fourth annual Robeson concert was announced for August 26, 1949, with the proceeds slated for the Harlem chapter of the Civil Rights Congress. The concert was broken up by force before it could even begin. It was the scene of one of the most frightening displays of racism and Nazi sentiment ever seen in America. The target was my grandfather.

A week before the concert the local press began to incite the public against Robeson with editorials and bold headlines: "ROBESON AND HIS FOLLOWERS ARE UNWELCOME"; "ROBESON CONCERT HERE AIDS SUBVERSIVE UNIT." The president of the Peekskill Chamber of Commerce issued a public statement condemning the concert, and the Junior Chamber of Commerce followed suit, attacking the concert as un-American and urging "group action to discourage it." The public mind was excited—especially the local Ku Klux Klan element and the conservative veterans' associations. Leonard Rubenfield was the assistant district attorney for Westchester County and chaired the local Veterans Council, including the American Legion. He called a meeting to devise a plan of action to stop the concert, and members voted to lead a protest demonstration across the grounds during the concert. Veterans from neighboring towns would be asked to join.

Talk of violence filled the air. It was so strong that a group of local residents sent a telegram to state authorities, including Rubenfield's superior, the county district attorney, asking for police protection for the concert. The matter was passed right back to the local Peekskill authorities, who were openly or quietly supporting the protests. The state police responded that no unusual circumstances were expected.

These developments mirrored a wave of reaction that was spreading across the country. The press always seemed to set the tone. Talk

of peace and cooperation with the Soviet Union was portrayed as tantamount to treason. Criticism of America's racism at home was considered ungrateful. Warnings about the dangers of domestic fascism were touted as the making of a communist plot. The bottom line was, "If you don't like America, leave and go to Russia." My grandfather had his fingers on the pulse of America, but he had no idea of the violence and hate that were about to be unleashed against him at Peekskill.

The concert was scheduled to begin at eight o'clock. By seven o'clock about fifty carloads of anti-Robeson demonstrators had arrived at the picnic grounds. Several hundred more came on foot. The official protest parade was led by the head of the American Legion and the Westchester county clerk—a public servant. They barricaded the entrance to the concert grounds with a truck and a wall of huge stones, trapping the early arrivals inside. The protest grew, and the crowd became an angry mob.

One of the mob sent a false report inside to the concertgoers that a fight had broken out at the entrance. Twenty-five men rushed up from the bandstand area. They were confronted by the barricades and a mob of three hundred. The mob attacked, and several of the men were badly injured. Another group of concertgoers came to their rescue, and forty-two strong, they formed a human wall to hold off the mob from charging inside, where mostly women and children were gathered at the bandstand. A barrage of rocks and bottles smashed against their bodies, but they stood firm. . . . And then an incessant din from the mob:

"No one of you leave here alive!"
"You came in, you don't get out!"
"We're going to get Robeson!"
Half an hour passed. My grandfather was scheduled to arrive, and the mob knew it. Night began to fall, and the ominous glow of burning Klan crosses lit the perimeter of the concert area. Outside, cars full of people arriving for the concert were stoned and forced to turn back. Men, especially Blacks, were dragged from their cars and beaten. Empty cars were smashed and overturned. A soldier

on his way to call the state police for help had to drag a Black man from the clutches of a gang of White youths who were beating him and screaming, "Kill him! Let's finish him off!"

Meanwhile, Paul arrived at the train station in Peekskill, unaware of the violence at the concert grounds. Close friends rushed to the station to intercept him, fully aware that bands of youths were rallying in the streets to cries of "Lynch Robeson!" The friends rushed Paul to their waiting car, laid him on the back seat, covered him with potato sacks, and drove to the safety of their nearby home.

The mob was also on the lookout for my parents, who had been married just two months before. Their marriage had particularly excited the venom of local Klan and Nazi sympathizers now on the rampage. Fortunately, my mother was ill that morning, and my parents had decided to forgo the drive to Peekskill. Had they gone, they could well have been killed or brutally mauled. A group of local thugs was awaiting their arrival—with an accurate description of their car.

During the height of the riot, a car of the same description was spotted. Inside rode a Black man and a White women just passing through. They were immediately surrounded and pulled from the car. Just as the mob was about to set upon them, a young White man stepped forward and said, "Stop! They're not the ones." To the astonishment of the young couple the mob disappeared as quickly as it had gathered.

Back at the entrance to the concert grounds, the human wall holding back the mob was taking a brutal beating. Finally the mob charged, one thousand strong. Realizing the futility of resisting, the men fled to the bandstand. They surrounded the women and children there and began to sing "The Star Spangled Banner" and "God Bless America." They watched a scene unfold that was shockingly reminiscent of early scenes in Nazi Germany. The mob built a huge bonfire and burned every book, pamphlet, and sheet of music in sight. They circled the fire screaming obscenities and tossing smashed chairs into the fire.

Finally, at 10 P.M., the state police arrived.

The mob dispersed; not a single arrest was made.

Many local residents were outraged the next day when they discovered what had happened. 350 people met and formed the Westchester Committee of Law and Order. They invited Paul to return for a concert. Demands for a full investigation were immediately dispatched to Governor Thomas Dewey, who turned a deaf ear. In Harlem, the Civil Rights Congress held a huge rally; three thousand people jammed into the Golden Gate Ballroom to hear Paul speak, and two thousand stood and listened outside. The reaction in Harlem was electrifying. Even the top Black gangsters in Harlem offered their full support to Paul.

Bumpy Johnson, the king of Harlem's gangster world, asked my grandfather if there was anything he could to do help. He offered to settle the score at Peekskill. Bumpy offered Paul protection any time he was in need and did actually provide him with bodyguards for years. My grandfather came to know Bumpy well, and they spent many evenings playing chess together and analyzing world politics. The two developed the greatest mutual respect and admiration.

The second concert was announced for September 4. Reports circulated that fifty thousand would protest the concert this time. The day of the concert, twenty-five hundred concertgoers volunteered to form a human wall to protect and encircle the concert audience of twenty-five thousand. Inside on the bandstand another human wall was formed, mostly of veterans, to protect Paul when he sang. There were confirmed reports of snipers with telescopic sights in the surrounding hills. Outside, hundreds of protesters were clustered along the roads leading into the concert grounds shouting epithets and chanting, "You'll get in; you won't get out! We'll kill you!" State troopers alongside openly joined in the chanting.

The concert began on schedule despite scattered violence as cars entered the grounds. Finally, Paul rose to sing, surrounded by a phalanx of men ready to give their lives to protect him. The moment was filled with tension . . .

182

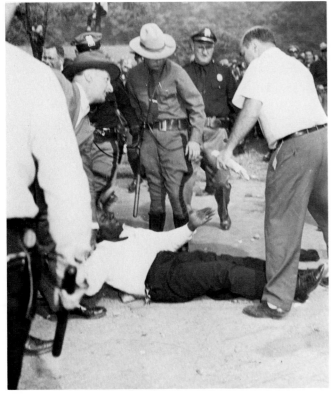

Eugene Ballard, first Black aviator in World War I, being attacked during concert at Peekskill, New York, September 4, 1949. (Courtesy of *Daily World*.)

Leaving concert at Peekskill, New York, August 26, 1949. (Courtesy of UPI.)

Leaving concert at Peekskill, New York, August 26, 1949. (Courtesy of UPI.)

184

Peekskill Concert, August 26, 1949. (Courtesy of *Daily News*.)

Peekskill Concert, August 26, 1949. (Courtesy of *Daily News*.)

but also with defiance and pride. Paul showed no fear, though death could have come at any moment. The crowd sensed it all. Outside, the protesters tried to drown out the applause of the crowd.

Paul's voice rose in song and rolled across the hills, drowning the sounds of protest. The people were filled with a human spirit so great and lifted so high that nothing could frighten or deter them, such was Paul's power. At that very moment, hundreds of miles away in Tallahassee, Florida, six Klan crosses burned, each with a sign that read, "We protest Paul Robeson and Communism." In Valadosta, Florida, an effigy of Robeson was hanged by the side of a road and burned.

As the concert ended, the mob outside and the state troopers became a single pack. For several miles they lined the roads leading out with stockpiles of rocks and bottles at their feet. A reporter from a Black paper, *The New York Age*, described the scene:

I still hear the frenzied roar of the crowds, the patter of stone against glass and flesh. I hear the wails of women, the impassioned screams of children, the jeers and taunts of wild-eyed youths. I still smell the sickening odor of blood flowing from freshly opened wounds, gasoline fumes from autos and buses valiantly trying to carry their human targets out of range of bricks, bottles, bottles and stones. I still feel the violence, the chaos which penetrated the air.[12]

There were many other similar eyewitness accounts:

As I drove out on the paved highway, a State Trooper slowed up the speed of our car. . . . Then a shower of rocks and pop bottles hit our car and one broke the windshield showering glass over the three of us. . . . There were State Troopers and uniformed police in great numbers all along the road, but they did absolutely nothing to prevent the violence."[13]

One woman described how

a group of hoodlums came directly in front of the bus and threw a huge boulder in. This boulder struck my left hand and when I looked down I saw the third joint of my middle finger was barely hanging by one tendon. Witnessing this incident were State Troopers who were laughing. As the stones kept coming, all I could think was: This is not America. This is Nazi Germany. I don't want to live like this.[14]

Reports of the Peekskill riots traveled around the globe. In America, only the politically courageous dared raise their voices in protest. Eleanor Roosevelt, the former first lady, was among many prominent people who felt compelled to speak out. "I dislike everything Paul Robeson is now saying," she said to the press. "I still believe, however, that if he wants to give a concert or speak his mind in public no one should prevent him from doing so."[15] An open letter defending Paul Robeson was sent to the press across the country from twenty-three leading personalities in the arts, among them Oscar Hammerstein II, Uta Hagen, Henry Fonda, Judy Holliday, and Moss Hart.

An investigation was ordered by Governor Dewey and conducted by the same authorities who had given their tacit support to the anti-Robeson protests. The report completely absolved the protesters and state police of any wrongdoing. The governor then ordered the investigation to proceed and determine whether the concert was "initiated and sponsored for the purpose of deliberately inciting disorder and a breach of the peace, and whether it was part of the Communist strategy to foment racial and religious hatreds." The victim was being made to appear the criminal. The press followed suit.

Paul spoke out in meeting after meeting to thousands who wanted to uphold his right to speak his mind and sing. "I shall take my voice wherever there are those who want to hear the melody of freedom or the words that might inspire hope and courage in the face of despair and fear. My weapons are peaceful, for it is only by peace that peace can be attained. The song of freedom must prevail."[16]

The pressure and efforts to silence Paul were reaching a climax.

Peekskill Concert, September 4, 1949.
(Courtesy of *Daily News.*)

Peekskill Concert, September 4, 1949.
(Courtesy of *Daily News.*)

In concert at Peekskill, with Larry Brown at the piano, September 4, 1949. (Courtesy of AP.)

Aerial view of Peekskill concert grounds and perimeter of defense, September 4, 1949. (Courtesy of UPI.)

Escort to safety after Peekskill concert, September 4, 1949. (Courtesy of UPI.)

Peekskill concert, September 4, 1949. (Courtesy of *Daily News.*)

Peekskill concert, September 4, 1949. (Courtesy of *Daily News*.)

Peekskill concert, August 26, 1949. (Courtesy of *Daily News*.)

Peekskill concert, September 4, 1949. (Courtesy of *Daily News*.)

Press conference day after Peekskill concert, August 27, 1949. (Courtesy of *Daily News*.)

192

Press conference day after Peekskill concert, August 27, 1949. (Courtesy of *Daily News*.)

Madison Square Garden, New York, 1949. (Courtesy of Julius Lazarus.)

I'm in the headlines and they're saying all manner of things about me such as "enemy" of the land of my birth, "traitor" to my country, "dangerous radical" and that I am an "ungrateful" cur. But they can't say that I am not 100 percent for my people. The American press has set out on its own campaign of deliberate misquotation and distortion of the things I say and do, trying to set my people against me, but they can't win because what I say is the unadulterated truth, which cannot be denied. . . .

I have asked myself just what Negro people am I fighting for. The big Negroes take it that I am fighting for them, and since they're comfortable and living good, they don't want too much fighting or things said that might prove embarrassing to their positions. My travels abroad, however, have shown me what and whom I am fighting for. During my travels, I met native Africans, West Indians, Chinese, East Indians and other Dark people who are fighting for the same thing —freedom from bondage . . . of imperialist Wall Street, the bankers and the plantation bosses. . . . The big Negro wants somebody to fight for him, but his objectives are purely selfish. . . .

I must fight for every Negro, wherever he may be.[17]

Leading delegation to demand repeal of indictments against twelve Communist leaders, Washington, D.C., October 12, 1949. (Courtesy of *Daily World*.)

194

Harlem, early 1950s. (Courtesy of *Daily World*.)

In the wake of events at Peekskill, the threat of violence arose wherever a Paul Robeson concert or meeting was announced. But my grandfather refused to bend—he would not be silenced, no matter what the price. The constitutional guarantees of freedom of speech and assembly were at stake. For years, since World War II, Paul had warned of the dangers of an American brand of fascism. Now he watched it unfold . . . and take singular aim at him. The press continued to fan the flames of anti-Robeson hysteria.

Before the Peekskill riots, the Council on African Affairs had arranged a series of concerts and meetings for Paul around the country. But he came under intense pressure from various sources to soften his stance or cancel the tour. Many feared for Paul's life. The first stops scheduled were in Pittsburgh, Akron, and Cincinnati. As soon as Paul's plans were announced to the press, sinister forces began maneuvering, and before Paul arrived in each city, contracts for the rented halls were canceled. The owners succumbed to every manner of threat, often from the FBI, and not a single owner could be found willing to rent a hall for a Robeson concert.

My grandfather continued on to Chicago, where he received a warm welcome and the Black churches flung their doors open to him. Reporters and photographers followed his every move in Chicago, but not a word appeared anywhere in the press. A curtain of silence was being drawn tight.

Meanwhile, the owners of the stadium in Los Angeles—Paul's next stop—were being intimidated into canceling the stadium contract for Paul's concert. Death threats were even made against the life of the concert's sponsor. At the same time, a well-financed advertising campaign was launched by the Motion Picture Alliance for the Preservation of American Ideals accusing Paul of being a communist and un-American and advising the public to boycott the concert. The Los Angeles City Council met and passed a resolution banning the concert. They broadcast their decision continually over the radio, telling people to stay home if they didn't want violence. All this was to no avail—sixteen thousand people attended the concert.

In other cities the harassment continued. Articles would appear in the press right before Paul's scheduled arrival, inciting readers to repeat the actions of Peekskill. Paul began to give lengthy press conferences, sometimes two and three hours long. He even invited outside people to monitor his statements to the press. But not a word appeared in the papers. "Few people in the United States remained neutral toward Robeson," Paul's biographer Marie Seton later wrote. "They took their place for or against him. Among Negroes, certain businessmen and professionals turned against him. For them, as for their white counterparts, Robeson was a man to be marked down and hounded into submission by every means short of physical martyrdom, which appeared too dangerous since nobody could gauge what percentage of 16 million Negroes in America would rise in wrath if Robeson was arrested or mauled; but everything short of this was tried in the next few years."[18]

An economic boycott was instituted, and Robeson records were eliminated from record stores, cutting off a substantial source of his income. The press pulled out all stops in its attempt to villify Robeson, and by 1951 any journalist or commentator who did not criticize Robeson in harsh terms when doing a story on him could count on losing his or her job. NBC-TV actually prohibited Paul from ever appearing in their studios. This policy was precipitated by an invitation from Eleanor Roosevelt for Paul to appear on her program "The Negro in American Political Life," as part of a panel discussion. Several major newspapers, the Hearst chain in particular, loudly protested the announcement of Paul's scheduled TV appearance, and the vice-president of NBC-TV issued a statement canceling the program: "We are doubtful that Robeson will ever appear on NBC except under circumstances beyond our control. . . . If he were to become the accredited candidate of a political party, we might be forced to give him free time."[19]

The repression against Paul was steadily escalating. FBI surveillance was now open; they followed him to meetings, concerts, home—wherever he went. Paul's life became an open book; to live otherwise invited legal disaster. In the summer of 1950, the State Department learned that Paul was making plans to go abroad for concert tours. In July, high-ranking officials in government decided to put a stop to Paul's travels. On July 28, State Department agents, under orders from Secretary of State Dean Acheson, visited Paul and demanded that he surrender his unexpired passport. Of course, he refused. The next week, the State Department announced to the press that Paul Robeson's passport had been canceled. An editorial in a major New York paper said of the situation:

The State Department acts correctly in cancelling Paul Robeson's passport. . . . The question is whether the issuance of the passport . . . is in the best national interest. And in Mr. Robeson's case, the State Department is simply stating in full authority that his projected travels are not to the best American interest. Mr. Robeson will have to stay at home.

Paul Robeson's record as an agitator . . . is well known. His plans for an extensive series of appearances at European "peace" rallies, followed by ideological traipsings through Africa and Australia . . . that is something this country can well be spared. The State Department has acted effectively. . . . This is not the sort of unofficial ambassador we want roaming the world under American passport. . . . Paul Robeson need not think he can have citizenship both ways. The State Department's realism will be acclaimed by every firm-minded American.[20]

The passports of Essie and Paul, Jr., were canceled next. The Robeson family was a prisoner in their own country—accused of no crime. The case was unprecedented in American history. Never had an artist been so feared. "The persecution of Paul Robeson by the Government . . . has been one of the most contemptible happenings in modern history," wrote W. E. B. Du Bois. "He is without doubt today, as a person, the best known American on earth to the largest number of human beings. His voice is known in Europe, Asia and Africa, in the West Indies and South America and in the islands of the seas. . . . Only in his native land is he without honor and rights."

My grandfather immediately instituted a legal suit to regain his passport. The State Department maintained in their legal briefs that the passport denial was based on Paul's long-standing activity against colonialism in Africa. Paul was offered his passport back if he signed affidavits affirming or denying his membership in the Communist party. Paul refused, as a matter of principle.

For the next eight years the FBI relentlessly hounded my grandfather. The economic boycott was intensified—not a single concert hall or recording studio in the country was accessible to Paul. If an owner of a studio or hall did entertain the thought, the FBI immediately paid a visit and ended that. Denied any outlet to work, unable to travel, trapped in his own country rather than exiled from it, Paul's income dwindled from a hundred thousand dollars to five thousand in less than one year. Honors were withdrawn, and friends disappeared. Paul, once a national hero, was now an outcast.

The McCarthy era had settled in, and to be labeled a communist meant certain disaster and possibly jail for any individual. Literally, anything from going to a Paul Robeson concert to signing a petition to ban the atom bomb was grounds for reprisals. Many reacted with fear and informed on friends or associates to save themselves; others watched in silence as lives and careers were shattered. Some even committed suicide rather than appear before the dreaded McCarthy committees holding continuous hearings in Washington. People were considered guilty by association with Paul, and many, unable to take the pressure, turned against him. He noticed that some friends now crossed the street to avoid having to face him in public and the possibility of being seen and having to face persecution for showing open friendship for him.

But there were also many courageous people who stood by my grandfather and their principles at great personal sacrifice. Paul's bedrock of strength and support was the Black community, and the Black church flung its doors open to Paul, as it had immediately after Peekskill. Paul was a living symbol, for Black people, of the fight for dignity, peace, and freedom. A worldwide campaign was begun in England to pressure the American government into returning Paul's passport. Meanwhile, his case made its tortuous way through the courts.

Marathon demonstration in support of Fair Employment Practices Commission Bill pending in Congress, Washington, D.C., May 24, 1950.

Civil Rights Congress rally, Madison Square Garden, New York, June 28, 1950. (Courtesy of AP.)

Harlem rally sponsored by the Council on African Affairs, July 4, 1950. (Courtesy of AP.)

Leaving district court, after the State Department's refusal to grant passport, with Paul, Jr. (partially obstructed), and Lloyd Brown, longtime friend and biographer, Washington, D.C., August 16, 1955. (Courtesy of UPI.)

The American people will someday take pride in the fact that at a time when the United States government was the driving force behind the oppression of hundreds of millions of people throughout the world, it was boldly called before the bar of world opinion by progressive Americans who exposed its pretensions of "democracy" and proved it guilty of genocide within its own borders. [21]

Presenting petition to secretary general of United Nations, charging the United States with genocide against Black Americans, December 17, 1951. (Courtesy of *Daily Worker*.)

Picket in defense of Paul's freedom of speech, New York, mid-1950s. (Courtesy of Dorothy Hunton Collection.)

Concert before forty thousand at Peace Arch Park, United States–Canada border, Washington, May 18, 1952. (Courtesy of Paul Robeson, Jr.)

With Essie at peace rally, Randall's Island, New York, August 21, 1952. (Courtesy of *Daily News.*)

Essie testifying before Joseph McCarthy's senate committee, Washington, D.C., July 8, 1953. (Courtesy of UPI.)

May Day rally, Union Square, New York, 1954. (Courtesy of *Daily News.*)

My grandfather stood his ground, defiant and proud. "I will not retreat," he said, "not even one thousandth part of one inch." In 1952 he accepted an invitation to sing in Canada, right across the border from the state of Washington. But Paul was refused entry, though no passport is required of United States citizens to enter Canada. President Truman had issued an unprecedented executive order forbidding Paul to leave the United States and authorizing border guards to shoot on sight, if necessary. Undaunted, Paul gave his concert . . . on the American side of the border. Forty thousand people gathered in Peace Arch Park on both sides of the border and listened spellbound to an impassioned Robeson concert.

Paul continued in every way he could to break through the curtain of silence, though at times it seemed impossible. In Chicago in 1953, he did manage to turn the tables. A concert was organized in a major Black church, but at the last minute the bank threatened to foreclose on the church's mortgage if Paul sang there, and the concert was canceled. However, Paul's voice could not be silenced. A small group of street-corner speakers offered him the use of their platform in Washington Park, and twenty-five thousand people came to hear Paul sing there. The subtle symbolism of the spirituals, forged during slavery, was not lost on the crowd. . . .

> Go down, Moses,
> Way down in Egypt's land.
> Tell ol' Pharoah
> To let my people go!
>
> Didn't my Lord deliver Daniel,
> Daniel, Daniel?
> Didn't my Lord deliver Daniel,
> And why not every man?

In 1955, the historic Bandung Conference met in Indonesia. This was the precursor of today's nonaligned-nation movement. It was the first time that the nations of the Third World came together to develop a common course against their oppression. Each nation sent its head of state or foreign minister. My grandfather was invited to address the conference. He applied for a passport again, but it was denied. Unable to travel, he sent a tape-recorded message to the Bandung Conference.

The same year, the Council on African Affairs was forced to disband as a result of intense government harassment. The Council had been chaired by my grandfather and Dr. Du Bois since its founding in 1937. The Council, which included other dedicated and brilliant activists like Alphaeus Hunton, had played a monumental role in fighting for African independence and instilling the pride of Africa in Afro-Americans.

The following year, in the summer of 1956, Paul was subpoenaed to testify before HUAC. Many people in the arts had already testified. Some had given in and testified against their friends; others had defied the committee and faced jail and financial ruin. Over the years the twisted politics of the cold war had made Paul's name synonymous with un-Americanism and treason. One congressional committee went so far as to establish that ownership of a Robeson record was proof of Communist ties and treasonous ideas.

The press was out in full force when my grandfather entered the HUAC hearing room, accompanied by his attorney. He was well aware of the likelihood of a prison term if he refused to cooperate. From the outset, he was defiant. The chairman questioned Paul about his identity. Finding that absurd, Paul demanded to know by whom he was being addressed. The committee was shocked and enraged by Paul's arrogance and fearlessness. They were used to meeker and more timid witnesses. The session was long and stormy. Paul argued incessantly that the real un-Americans were those bigots who lynched and brutalized Black people. He demanded that the American government send troops down South to protect Black people from violence rather than rattle sabers against the Soviet Union. And he steadfastly refused, as a matter of principle, to say whether he was a communist.

By the time the hearing ended, the committee voted to cite my grandfather for contempt—certain grounds for imprisonment. Fortunately the contempt citation never went past a vote for the record. Perhaps the government was too frightened of the consequences of imprisoning Paul Robeson.

After seven long years, my grandfather began to break through the curtain of silence. In the spring of 1957, he gave the most unusual concert of his career—by long-distance phone. Organizers of the influential London-based worldwide campaign to restore Paul's passport had long requested the State Department tó allow Paul to travel to England for concerts. Now they decided to use the new trans-Atlantic phone cables to defy the American government. In May, the Saint Pancras Town Hall in London was sold out, with hundreds turned away, and my grandfather gave a twenty-minute recital by telephone. His voice came in over the speakers, crisp and clear, from a New York studio where the family and a few close friends had gathered. I was four years old, too young to remember much but the tremendous excitement. The American press in London was invited but ignored the event. Paul Robeson's voice could not be stilled.

In the fall of 1957 Paul made a stunning comeback in a series of sell-out concerts in California. Finally, he was reestablishing his concert career.

Later that year, my grandfather's book *Here I Stand* was published by an independent company, Othello Associates, headed by Lloyd Brown, my grandfather's collaborator on the book; Stanley Levison; and my father. For political reasons, no commercial publisher would touch the book, and upon release it was officially ignored by the press. The book summarized my grandfather's beliefs, and among other things it was a prophecy of the coming decade of Black power:

Dedication to the Negro people's welfare is one side of the coin: the other is *independence*. Effective Negro leadership must rely upon and be responsive to no other control than the will of their people. We have allies—important allies—among our white fellow citizens, and we must ever seek to draw them closer to us and gain many more. But the Negro people's movement must be led by Negroes. . . . Good advice is good no matter what the source and help is needed and appreciated from wherever it comes, but Negro action cannot be decisive if the advisors and helpers hold the guiding reins. For no matter how well-meaning other groups may be, the fact is our interests are secondary, at best, with them.[22]

The 1950s were probably the most difficult time in my grandfather's life. His life was in jeopardy on numerous occasions during these years, and bodyguards often accompanied him in public. But though the political pressures were enormous, the personal pressures were far more complex and difficult to handle. All of a sudden, his public and artistic life came to a standstill—he went from tremendous activity to unending inactivity. The effect of this on any artist or public figure would be devastating, and for Paul Robeson, with his extraordinary creative energies, the impact was almost unbearable.

Of course, initially a person in this position experiences a rush of activism to defend and resist; but eight years is a long time for a career and a way of life to be upended. In addition, the atmosphere in America was repressive and unpleasant. The fears brought on by McCarthy's reign generated a kind of inward turning among many, and people became guarded and very careful about what they said to whom. Suspicion developed as a personal trait where it had not existed before.

My grandfather bent under the pressures, but he did not break. There was a kind of unconquerable spirit within him to struggle on. What is incredible to me about the whole experience is that he never turned bitter, though he had every reason to be. In looking back over the years of his career, a kind of sinister pattern emerges. The era of 1939 to 1946 was a time when my grandfather reached the pinnacle of fame and fortune. The era that followed immediately, from 1947 to 1958, was a decade of intense persecution, both overt and covert, that resulted in nonperson status for him. All of a sudden he was blotted out from the public eye and public mind, isolated by the silence. It was as though the hand of Big Brother reached out and snatched this giant of a man from his perch, where he held the whole world in his hands. Someone, it seems, decided that he must be stopped at all costs.

I was born in 1953, in the midst of these difficult and sometimes traumatic years. Though adults have their way of shielding children from the harsh realities of life, a sense of trouble often pervaded the house, and I learned quickly that it was not always my place to ask why. But despite the pressures that often engulfed the family, these were happy years for me, and they were the years when we were most together as a family. I realize now that had my grandfather not been hemmed in by the political realities of McCarthyism, I would probably have seen much less of him during my childhood. I am grateful that I grew up knowing and appreciating him first as Grandpa, the beautiful and gentle giant who just engulfed me with his presence and was so unusual and delightful to be with. He cast his spell over me, and I was affected by him more profoundly because I loved him first as my grandfather and then as the great and famous man he was.

> *ROBESON:* *I stand here struggling for the rights of my people to be full citizens in this country and they are not. They are not in Mississippi and they are not . . . in Washington. . . . You want to shut up every Negro who has the courage to stand up and fight for the rights of his people. . . . That is why I am here today. . . .*
>
> *MR. SCHERER:* *Why do you not stay in Russia?*
>
> *MR. ROBESON:* *Because my father was a slave, and my people died to build this country and I am going to stay here and have a part of it just like you. And no fascist-minded people will drive me from it. Is that clear?*[23]

HUAC Testimony 1956

Testifying before HUAC, Washington, D.C., June 12, 1956. (Courtesy of United Press International.)

For the past several years a vicious effort has been made to destroy my career. Hall-owners, sponsors and even audiences have been intimidated. Recently in Chicago, 15,000 persons who wanted to attend one of my concerts had to assemble in a park because the hall owner had been threatened.

The outrageous denial of my passport bars me from accepting contracts to appear in England, France, China and many other lands.

Although I have recorded for nearly every major recording company and sold millions of records both here and abroad, these companies refuse to produce any new recordings for me.

What is the meaning of this? It is an attempt to gag artistic expression to dictate whom the people shall hear and what they shall hear.[24]

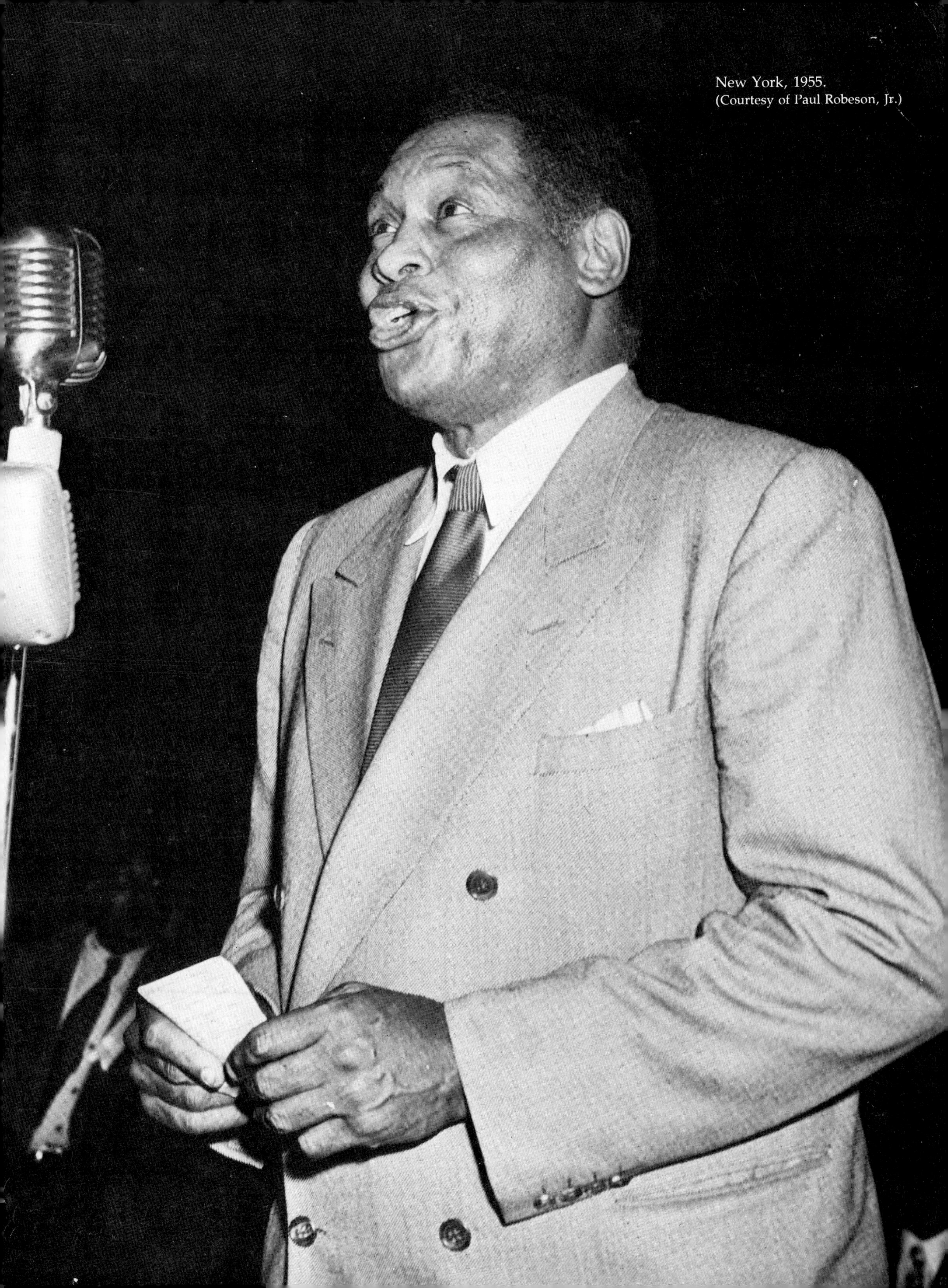

New York, 1955.
(Courtesy of Paul Robeson, Jr.)

HUAC, after voting to cite Paul for contempt, Washington, D.C., June 12, 1956. (*Left to right,* Edwin Willis; James Frazier, Jr.; Clyde Doyle; Morgan Moulder; Francis Walter, chairman; Gordon H. Scherer; Bernard Kearney; and Frank Tavener, Jr. (Courtesy of UPI.)

In concert, with accompanist Alan Booth, Parkchester, New York, 1956. (Courtesy of Julius Lazarus.)

With Alphaeus Hunton, being escorted past anti-Soviet demonstration to annual celebration of Russian revolution, November 13, 1956, New York. (Courtesy of UPI.)

With Alphaeus and Dorothy Hunton and W. E. B. DuBois after Alphaeus's release from federal prison, New York, 1955. (Courtesy of Dorothy Hunton Collection.)

With accompanist Alan Booth, New York, 1956. (Courtesy of *Freedomways*.)

Concert at A.M.E. Zion Church, pastored by Paul's brother Ben, Harlem, 1958. (Courtesy of Julius Lazarus.)

"How long, O Lord, how long?" —that ancient cry of the oppressed is often voiced these days. . . . How long? . . . As long as we permit it. . . . Negro action can be decisive. . . . We ourselves have the power to end the terror and win for ourselves peace and security. . . .

We have the power of numbers, the power of organization and the power of spirit. . . . Above all we have the duty to bring the strength and support of our entire community to defend the lives and property of each individual family. . . . The law itself will move a hundred times quicker when it is apparent that the power of numbers has been called forth. . . .

For Negro action to be effective . . . it must be mass action. . . . Mass action —in political life and elsewhere —is Negro power in motion: and it is the way to win.[25]

(Opposite page) New York, 1958. (Courtesy of Paul Robeson, Jr.)

Harlem, 1955. (Courtesy of *Freedomways*.)

With newly regained passport, in lawyer Leonard Boudin's office, New York, May 1958. (Courtesy of *New York Times*.)

6
THE GENTLE GIANT RETURNS

The spring of 1958 ushered in the final touches to my grandfather's comeback after eight years of unprecedented persecution for his political beliefs and the crippling of his career as an artist.

This was due, in part, to a lessening of the cold-war policies that dominated American life during the 1950s. McCarthyism was tumbling from its rotten perch.

In May 1958, Paul gave two sell-out concerts back to back at New York's Carnegie Hall. It had been eleven years since his last concert there, and he thrilled the audiences with his still rich and colorful voice—he was "the same Paul."

The critics were overwhelmed. *Saturday Review* wrote, "The voice which has been his professional asset for singing, speaking and acting over a full thirty-five year span is still potent. . . . Robeson remains a man of magnificent vocal endowments with a highly cultivated sense of phrase and accent, a power of articulation second to none among his contemporaries." This praise was typical of the concert reviews. At the end of the second Carnegie Hall concert, Paul announced that the long, hard battle had finally been won—

he had his passport back and was free to travel once again. Another triumphant concert was given that same spring in the A.M.E. Zion church in Harlem, pastored by Paul's brother Ben. That was a momentous occasion for me: I was five, and it was the first time I heard my grandfather sing in public. I swelled with pride when he looked at me and sang my favorite song, "Sometimes I Feel Like a Motherless Child."

During the concert, my grandfather extended his deep gratitude and warm thanks to the Black community—especially the church—for opening their arms and doors to him at a time when people faced political persecution for mere association with him and his ideas.

After his nine-year absence, audiences the world over were clamoring for Paul's return. So in July 1958 he and Essie left New York for London, where a tumultuous welcome awaited them. He opened his English tour at London's Albert Hall to an enthusiastic overflow crowd. Benny Green, a noted English music critic, described Paul in concert that evening: "Robeson is one of the archetypal artists of the twentieth century. He is one of those all too rare people who can, through some miraculous alchemy of the spirit, reach out, and within the scope of a single gesture or phrase, touch the hearts of both the gallery-ites looking for a good time and the intellectuals probing for the Message. When he sings I hear the unsullied expression of the human spirit."

In August, my grandparents flew to Moscow, to a hero's welcome. The Soviet people had kept a special place in their hearts for this unsullied giant. Paul gave concerts, appeared on Moscow TV, and then took a trip to the Crimea, to a seaside resort near Yalta, where Paul and Essie joined the vacationing Premier Nikita Khrushchev for a friendly, informal visit.

Paul returned to London early in the fall and gave a historic recital in England's most majestic church, Saint Paul's Cathedral. He was the first layman ever to take the lectern at the cathedral. Four thousand people packed the church, and five thousand more stood outside and listened through loudspeakers. At the end of the concert Paul was literally mobbed by enthusiastic admirers and had to be rescued by police.

My grandparents were back in Moscow for New Year's 1959 . . . and then Paul fell ill. He was hospitalized with a circulatory disorder that was eventually diagnosed as a cerebral vascular disorder. By February, Paul's condition had improved. During his hospitalization, Essie had turned down an invitation from Glen Byam Shaw for Paul to appear in *Othello* in Stratford-upon-Avon, the town of Shakespeare's birth. Finally, the doctors relented with the stipulation that Paul rely on his voice and minimize physical activity. The news that Paul would appear in *Othello* traveled fast, and performances were sold out months in advance. Paul received great critical acclaim for his performance, though the 1944 Broadway production has remained unsurpassed to this day.

My grandfather was now sixty-one, and his health began to fail him. But he continued with concert tours of the British Isles, compelled by an inner drive to give of himself spiritually and artistically.

The world was swiftly changing, echoing many of Paul's prophecies of decades earlier. African nations were gaining their independence from European colonialism; revolution had triumphed in Cuba, making it the first socialist country of the Western Hemisphere; and the civil rights movement was building momentum in the Deep South. These events touched Paul deeply. He announced to the press that he was planning to travel to Africa and then to Cuba and the Caribbean. The American government bridled; the last thing in the world they wanted was a healthy, brilliant Paul Robeson in newly independent Africa, meeting Africans still fighting for liberation. The thought of Robeson in Cuba sent the same waves of fear through the State Department. Similar fears a decade earlier had led the State Department to revoke my grandfather's passport. The government's secret war against Paul Robeson was stepped up. Someday soon, perhaps, the full and sinister story will come to light and those responsible will be publicly branded and punished.

In November 1960, my grandparents flew to Australia, and Paul gave what turned out to be the last concert tour of his career. He traveled throughout Australia and New Zealand with great success. He embarrassed the Establishment there by openly talking about the oppression of the indigenous people by the Europeans. Some reporters admonished him for mixing in Australian politics, cautioning him to stick to singing. The tour was grueling for Paul, and he returned with Essie to London at the end of 1960, exhausted but in good spirits.

By the spring of 1961, my grandfather had entered a Moscow hospital. He was there when an invitation came from his longtime friend Kwame Nkrumah, prime minister of newly independent Ghana, to accept a post as director of the music department at the University of Ghana. The State Department went through elaborate pains to prevent the appointment, but in the end, my grandfather's health prevented him from accepting.

Paul spent the next two and a half years in Moscow, East Berlin, and London, often resting and going for treatments in hospitals and nursing homes. By this time, he had withdrawn from active public life, and Essie, forever instrumental in handling Paul's affairs, kept a rumor-mongering, hostile press at arm's length. In 1963 a vicious rumor circulated in the press that Paul was a broken and bitter man being held prisoner in an East German sanitorium. This was denied by the family, but the impression remained, fostered by the press.

My grandfather was a man of intense dignity, a quality that remained intact even as he grew older and his health failed. Paul was still every inch a fighter, and as always, he chose to exercise his inalienable right to determine his own image, refusing to allow the press to distort it according to their own biases. My grandfather chose retirement with dignity. He felt he could no longer maintain a public posture and be active as he had in his prime. But he was still the same Paul. He was simply worn by four long decades of struggle and active public life.

As these years passed, I grew to understand more and more who my grandfather was and to appreciate his significance. I was five years old when he and my grandmother left triumphantly for England in 1958, after winning back their passports. I remember vividly the day we saw them off at the airport and the sense of satisfaction it gave me, though I knew I would miss them.

The following year, I spent the most exciting summer in my life with my older brother, Dave, in London and Stratford-upon-Avon. We spent a fascinating two months with my grandparents during the time of my grandfather's last stage performances, in *Othello* in 1959. While he was in rehearsals and resting between performances, we spent the time with my grandmother, exploring London and Stratford, which she knew like the back of her hand.

My brother and I had the time of our lives, and when we returned home to Harlem, we had been opened to the wonders of travel and its mind-expanding qualities.

It was another four years before I saw my grandparents again. The family kept in contact with long letters, mostly from my grandmother, and phone calls on holidays and birthdays.

During these years I had very little concept of the stresses and strains my grandfather was undergoing. I knew only that he was sick and hospitalized on occasion. But I was growing fast and reading everything in sight.

Leaving New York for London after regaining passport, July 14, 1958. (Courtesy of Paul Robeson, Jr.)

219

With Doctor G. W. Brown during British concert tour, London, November 1958.

Relaxing during newspaper interview, Moscow, 1958. (Courtesy of *Freedomways*.)

On streets of Moscow, 1958. (Courtesy of *Freedomways*.)

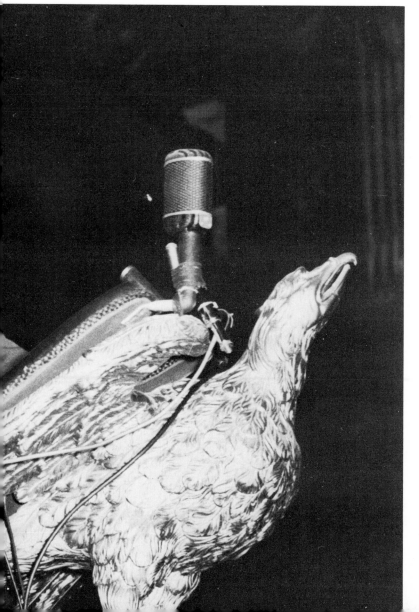

Saint Paul's Cathedral, London, October 12, 1958. (Courtesy of Julius Lazarus.)

Lenin Artek Pioneer Camp, Moscow, September 1958. (Courtesy of Sovfoto.)

The Stratford Company, 1959 Shakespeare season, Stratford-on-Avon, England, with Charles Laughton (*far left*). Clockwise: Peter Hall, Paul, Glen Byam Shaw, Sir Laurence Olivier, Harry Andrews, Dame Edith Evans, Mary Ure, Angela Baddeley, and Leslie Caron. (Courtesy of Roger Wood/Paul Robeson, Jr.)

Arrival in Moscow, December 1958. (Courtesy of Sovfoto.)

Othello, Stratford-on-Avon, 1959. (Courtesy of Anthony Armstrong-Jones.)

Othello, Stratford-on-Avon, 1959. (Courtesy of Anthony Armstrong-Jones.)

224

Stratford-on-Avon, 1959. (Courtesy of Julius Lazarus/
Paul Robeson, Jr.)

I learned that the essential character of a nation is determined not by the upper classes, but by the common people, and that the common people of all nations are truly brothers in the great family of mankind. . . . Even as I grew to feel more Negro in spirit, or African as I put it then, I also came to feel a sense of oneness with the white working people whom I came to know and love.

This belief in the oneness of humankind . . . has existed within me side by side with my deep attachment to the cause of my own race. Some people have seen a contradiction in this duality. . . . I do not think, however, that my sentiments are contradictory.[1]

Third World students greeting Paul on his arrival for World Youth Festival, Vienna, 1959. (Courtesy of Julius Lazarus.)

In concert, Paris, 1959. (Courtesy of Paul Robeson, Jr.)

Peace demonstration, Trafalgar Square, London, June 1959. (Courtesy of Paul Robeson, Jr.)

Moscow, 1960. (Courtesy of *Freedomways*.)

227

With workers at a bearing plant, Moscow, January 1960. (Courtesy of SovFoto.)

London, 1960. (Courtesy of Paul Robeson, Jr.)

228

Arrival in Berlin, 1960. (Courtesy of Paul Robeson, Jr.)

Celebration of Nigerian independence, London, September 1960. (Courtesy of Paul Robeson, Jr.)

Celebration of Nigerian independence, London, September 1960. (Courtesy of Paul Robeson, Jr.)

Concert on construction site of the Sydney Opera House during Paul's Australian tour, 1960. (Courtesy of Paul Robeson, Jr.)

With Essie during Australian tour, 1960. (Courtesy of Paul Robeson, Jr.)

Sydney, Australia, 1960. (Courtesy of Paul Robeson, Jr.)

With portrait of Patrice Lumumba presented at Patrice Lumumba Friendship University, Moscow, March 1961. (Courtesy of Paul Robeson, Jr.)

With students at Patrice Lumumba Friendship University, Moscow, March 1961. (Courtesy of SovFoto.)

Returning home to New York, after several months of medical treatment in East Berlin, December 18, 1963. (Courtesy of SovFoto.)

The winter of 1963 found my grandfather, at age sixty-five, in better health and spirits. In December, he and my grandmother decided to return home to New York to live out the remainder of their lives with family and close friends. They left East Berlin, where Paul had just completed several months of medical treatment, and flew to New York via London.

At the airport in New York the press was out in full force, poised for attack. But my family and a few close friends were there, and as Paul and Essie stepped off the plane we immediately surrounded them, partly to protect them from the onslaught of the press, whose members pressed around, cameras snapping, popping off all manner of hostile questions. The next day, true to form, the headline in the *New York Times* appeared: "Paul Robeson: Disillusioned Native Son." It didn't matter what my grandfather said or did; the press had a picture they wanted to paint.

My grandparents settled into the brownstone home on Jumel Terrace in Washington Heights they had purchased and lived in during the 1950s. For the next several months, public appearances were rare for Paul. He preferred the privacy of family and close friends.

In August 1964, Paul made his first public statement since his return home. It was the anniversary of the 1963 March on Washington; the "long, hot summer" was on, and in the Deep South the civil rights movement was taking the offensive with a massive voter-registration drive. My grandfather offered his support and inspiration to the struggle for Black liberation. The following month, he delivered the eulogy at the funeral of his close friend the long-time Harlem activist and city councilman Benjamin J. Davis, Jr.

Then, in the winter of 1965, Paul made two more public appearances, and he attended the funeral of Lorraine Hansberry, the gifted young author of *A Raisin in the Sun*.

In April 1965, *Freedomways* magazine sponsored a welcome-home birthday salute at the Americana Hotel in New York. It was attended by several thousand people, including numerous celebrities. This was my grandfather's first major public appearance since returning home. Everyone was anticipating Paul's speech, the climax and close of the evening's celebration—would they hear Paul sing, one last time? Even Paul didn't know, having decided to make that decision during his speech. He finally rose to the stage, and the audience surged to its feet with a standing ovation. Paul, deeply moved, delivered a touching speech. At the close he broke into song with the last verse of "Ol' Man River": "I keeps laughin' instead of cryin'; I must keep fightin' until I'm dyin'. And Ol' Man River, he just keeps rollin' along." The effect was electrifying.

Before the summer was over, my grandfather took off for California to speak and sing at several gatherings, but the strain was too much. He returned home exhausted and became terribly ill. He was hospitalized and almost died.

The next several months were emotionally painful and trying. For several years, my grandmother had been suffering from terminal cancer, and now her bout with death neared its end. Only the family and close friends were aware of her long sickness. One evening, after weeks of long hours visiting her at the hospital, my parents decided to have a serious talk with me and my brother Dave. I was a grown-up twelve at the time and Dave was fourteen. They told us that Nana was very ill and would certainly die; it was only a matter of time. I was devastated, and there was no comforting me as I cried myself to sleep that night. I was just beginning to identify with and understand the magnitude of her life, and my sense of loss went deep. She died the next day, December 12, 1965, on the eve of her sixty-ninth birthday.

Some of the pressure eased for Paul. But now he was alone, and our family moved into the Jumel Terrace brownstone with him. Meanwhile a search began for a new home where we could all live together comfortably. In the fall of 1966, we moved to a gigantic apartment on West 86th Street, where my grandfather lived with us for a year and a half.

And then, in 1968, he moved to Philadelphia to live with Marian, his youngest sister and the only remaining family member of his generation. The pressure of New York had been too great for Paul. There were very few people he chose to see; yet so many pressed about.

When we went out as a family, there was always an aggressive, though adoring, public for my grandfather to contend with. He wanted now to live a very quiet private life, and Philadelphia seemed a better place.

The next eight years were filled with a duality of feelings for my grandfather. There was the sadness of a great warrior sidelined by failing health and no longer able to do battle, yet the satisfaction of watching a growing militancy as the consciousness of Black Americans began to catch up with his own and the Third World solidified the independence that Paul had fought so hard and sacrificed so long for.

Paul's seclusion sparked many rumors— most commonly that he was now a bitter and broken man, that his life had turned into a tragedy of betrayal, like that of Shakespeare's Othello. Quite unnecessarily, his retirement was made a sinister mystery. "People should understand," he said in 1975, "that when I could be active I went here, there, and everywhere. What I wanted to do I did; what I wanted to say I said; and now that ill health has compelled my retirement I have decided to let the record speak for itself. As far as my basic outlook is concerned, everybody should know that I'm the same Paul Robeson and the viewpoint I expressed in my book *Here I Stand* has never changed."

Three days after Christmas 1975, Paul was admitted to the hospital after suffering a stroke. One month later, on the afternoon of January 23, 1976, at the age of seventy-seven, he passed on to the spirit world of the ancestors.

I was twenty-two when my grandfather died. His death had a profound impact on my life. It was like a ray of light that brought order to my life and pointed me safely in the proper direction along my path. His death is a marker for me, a point from which I now mark time.

The afternoon of his death is etched in my mind and brings back a deep personal sadness, because when he died, I was on my way to see him for what I knew would be the last time ever. I was on my way to my downtown Manhattan office by subway. I planned to leave the office and meet my father and take the train to Philadelphia, where my grandfather was hospitalized. Right there in the subway, a strange feeling hit me, and for no apparent reason, my gaze became fixed on the clock on the subway platform. The image of the hands of the clock—11:45 A.M.—was frozen in my mind, and I remember feeling puzzled about what I was feeling and why.

About fifteen minutes later, I arrived in my office. My mother was on the phone, to tell me that Grandfather had just died. I was stunned, though not surprised. I remembered the feeling I had in the subway and the frozen image of the clock's hands: 11:45. That was the moment he died. Something in me had felt him pass; of that I am sure.

Though I was prepared for my grandfather's death, we had never discussed as a family what it would be like when he died. I was not emotionally prepared for the crush of people and events. I found it all strangely ironic. All of sudden, in death, America seemed to wake up and pay tribute to Paul Robeson, after more than two decades of pretending that he didn't exist. It's rather crude how this country tends to accord its true heroes proper respect only in death.

The days that followed, leading up to the funeral, were emotionally revelatory for me. I was literally overwhelmed by the outpourings of love and respect that came from every corner of America and the world. For two days my grandfather's body was on view at Benta's Funeral Home in Harlem, and thousands of people, of all colors, beliefs, and walks of life, streamed in and out to pay their last respects to their fallen hero. I spent most of these two days right at Benta's, watching this mass of humanity come and go, and I was moved to tears on more than one occasion.

I had never experienced such an outpouring of love and dedication for one human being, and it made me feel proud and strong. There were derelicts who literally came in off the streets, dusted themselves off, and assumed their most respectful posture as they passed the open casket. Here, in one humble abode in Harlem, I felt and saw the span and stretch of my grandfather's life, the hope he sparked in others. He had created a tremendous sway over people, an influence that was almost religious. From these days, I learned that the true mark of greatness lies in one's effect on others. No experience in my life has moved me so or taught me more.

Greeting at airport from Marilyn and Paul, Jr., after arrival from London; New York, December 22, 1963. (Courtesy of UPI.)

Escort from airport with Paul, Jr., and Lloyd Brown, *far right*, New York, December 22, 1963. (Courtesy of UPI.)

Author, age ten, with Paul and Essie at airport, December 22, 1963. (Courtesy of *Daily News*.)

Author, age ten, with Essie at airport, New York, December 22, 1963. (Courtesy of *Daily News*.)

Since my return home from Europe some eight months ago I have declined to give any interviews or make any public statements. The fact is, I have been resting and recovering my health and strength after a rather prolonged illness. But while I am not yet able to resume public life and activities, I think that it is time I said a few words. . . .

I am, or course, deeply involved with the great upsurge of our people. . . . My heart has been filled with admiration for the many thousands of freedom fighters . . . who are waging the battle for civil rights . . . especially in the South. Along with the pride has been the great sorrow and righteous wrath we all shared when the evil forces of white supremacy brutally murdered the Birmingham children and some of our finest heroes, like Medgar Evers and the three young men of Mississippi.

For me there has also been the sorrow that I have felt upon returning home and experiencing the loss of persons who for many years were near and dear to me. . . .

"Many thousand gone . . ." but we, the living, are more firmly resolved: "No more driver's lash for me!"

When I wrote . . . in 1958 that "the time is now," Some people thought that perhaps my watch was fast . . . but most of us seem to be running on the same time—now. The power of Negro action, of which I then wrote, has changed from an idea to a reality. . . . The concept of mass militancy, mass action, is no longer deemed "too radical" in Negro life. The idea that Black Americans should see that the fight for a "free world" begins at home—a shock-

ing idea when expressed in Paris in 1949—no longer is challenged in our communities. . . . Today it is the Negro artist who does not speak out who is considered to be out of line. . . . It is good to see . . . these transformations. . . . There is more—much more—that needs to be done, of course, before we can reach our goals. But if we cannot as yet sing "Thank God almighty, we're free at last," surely we can all sing together: "Thank God almighty, we're moving!"[2]

House party with friends, New York, 1964. (Courtesy of Paul Robeson, Jr.)

Last major public appearance, welcome-home birthday salute sponsored by *Freedomways*, New York, April 1965. (Courtesy of Beuford Smith.)

With Essie and Diana Sands, *Freedomways* salute, New York, April 1965. (Courtesy of Beuford Smith.)

Though ill health has compelled my retirement, you can be sure that in my heart I go on singing:

But I keeps laughin' instead of cryin';
I must keep fightin' until I'm dyin'.
And Ol' Man River, he just keeps rollin'
   along![3]

Tape-recorded message   April   1973

(Opposite page) On steps of Jumel Terrace home, Harlem, 1965.

I am a singer and an actor. I am primarily an artist. Had I been born in Africa, I would have belonged, I hope, to that family which sings and chants the glories and legends of the tribe. I would have liked in my mature years to have been a wise elder, for I worship wisdom and knowledge of the ways of men.

Handwritten Note   1936

At airport during European tour after first concert ban in
United States, 1949. (Courtesy of Paul Robeson, Jr.)

There can be no greater tragedy than to forget one's origins and finish despised and hated by the people among whom one grew up. To have that happen would be the sort of thing to make me rise from my grave.

Handwritten Note   1936

(Opposite page) London, 1960. (Courtesy of Paul Robeson, Jr.)

Moscow, 1960.
(Courtesy of Paul Robeson, Jr.)

EPILOGUE

I discovered the following selection from the *Tao Tê Ching*, by Lao-tzu, among my grandfather's collection, after his death. It was his book, and this selection stood out because it was the only one he had marked. Though it was written more than two thousand years ago, I knew the moment I read it that it had touched him profoundly — like a mirror of his experiences — when he discovered it. I date that moment to the late 1950s, when my grandfather was under tremendous pressure; yet it harked back to the world view and the sources of knowledge he had been drawing upon in the 1930s.

Lao-tzu's images of water symbolize the spiritual lessons of my grandfather's life . . . and they are applicable to our social, political, and cultural realities, spanning the many and diverse worlds that his life spanned.

The weakest things in the world can overmatch
    the strongest things in the world.
Nothing in the world can be compared to water
    for its weak and yielding nature; yet in attacking the hard and the
    strong nothing proves better than it. For there is no alternative to it.
The weak can overcome the strong, and the yielding can overcome the hard:
This all the world knows but does not practice.
Therefore, the Sage says:
He who sustains all the reproaches of the country can be the master of the land;
He who sustains all the calamities of the country can be the king of the world.
These are words of truth,
Though they seem paradoxical.

Lenin Artek Pioneer Camp, Moscow, 1958.
(Courtesy of Paul Robeson, Jr.)

NOTES

CHAPTER 1

1. Paul Robeson, *Here I Stand* (New York: Othello Associates, 1957).
2. Commencement speech "The New Idealism," *The Targum* (New Brunswick, N.J.: Rutgers University, June 19, 1919).
3. Quoted in Marie Seton, *Paul Robeson* (London: Dobson Press, 1958).
4. Ibid.
5. *New York Telegram and Evening Mail*, May 7, 1924.
6. *New York World*, April 20, 1925.
7. Paul Robeson, "The Culture of the Negro," *The Spectator* (London), June 15, 1934.
8. Paul Robeson, *The New York Times*, May 18, 1930.
9. Letter from Eugene O'Neill to Mike Gold (author of *All God's Chillun Got Wings*), quoted in Barbara Gelb and Arthur Gelb, *O'Neill* (New York: Dell, 1962).
10. *Reynolds Illustrated News* (London), September 20, 1925.
11. Paul Robeson, *News Chronicle* (London), May 30, 1935.
12. Paul Robeson, "An Actor's Hopes and Wanderings," *The Messenger*, October 1924.
13. Paul Robeson, *Pearson's Weekly* (London), April 5, 1930.
14. *West Africa Review*, December 1936.
15. Paul Robeson, "How I Discovered Africa," *Freedom*, June 1953.
16. Comment to Sergei Eisenstein, quoted in Seton, *Paul Robeson*.
17. Manuscript text of Albert Hall speech, London, June 24, 1937.

CHAPTER 2

1. Paul Robeson, "What I Want from Life," *Royal Screen Pictorial* (London), April 1935.
2. *London Evening Standard*, June 12, 1930.
3. *Philadelphia Tribune*, November 2, 1933.
4. *London Observer*, July 29, 1934.
5. Interview by Ben Davis, Jr., *The Sunday Worker*, May 10, 1936.
6. *Los Angeles Evening Herald and Express*, May 13, 1936.
7. *Film Pictorial*, March 6, 1937.
8. *London Evening News*, September 19, 1936.
9. *Film Weekly*, May 23, 1936.
10. Interview, *London News Chronicle*, November 8, 1937.
11. Interview, *London News Chronicle*, November 1, 1938.
12. Interview, *Daily Worker* (London), November 24, 1937.
13. *Glasgow Record*, November 1, 1938.
14. *Afro-American*, May 24, 1941.

15. *PM*, November 14, 1942.

CHAPTER 4

1. Interview by Eugene Gordon, *Sunday Worker*, June 4, 1939.
2. Quoted in Marie Seton, *Paul Robeson* (London: Dobson Press, 1958).
3. Interview with Julia Dorn, Theatre Arts Committee, July 1939.
4. Interview with Richard Davis, *Milwaukee Journal*, October 20, 1941.
5. Interview with W. R. Titterton, *London Daily Herald*, July 11, 1930.
6. Excerpts from speech at Booker T. Washington School, New Orleans, October 29, 1942 (Paul Robeson Collection).
7. Address before the Herald Tribune Forum, 1943.
8. Paul Robeson quoted in Marvin Rosenberg, *Masks of Othello* (Berkeley, University of California Press, 1961).
9. Margaret Webster, quoted in Marie Seton, *Paul Robeson* (London: Dobson Press, 1958).
10. Helen Eager article, *Boston Traveler*, September 21, 1943.
11. *New York Herald Tribune*, 1944.
12. *New York Journal-American*, 1944.
13. *New York World-Telegram*, 1944.
14. Comments on *Othello*, delivered in concert.
15. Paul Robeson, "Some Reflections on Othello and the Nature of Our Times," *American Scholar*, 1945.

CHAPTER 5

1. Larry Brown, quoted in Marie Seton, *Paul Robeson* (London: Dobson Press, 1958).
2. *Philadelphia Inquirer*, March 16, 1947.
3. Paul Robeson, quoted in Seton, *Paul Robeson*.
4. Paul Robeson, quoted in Seton, *Paul Robeson*.
5. *Philadelphia Tribune*, September 24, 1946.
6. Paul Robeson, testimony before the Senate hearings on the Mundt-Nixon Bill, June 1948.

7. Speech delivered at the Paris Peace Conference, April 1949.
8. *Afro-American*, April 1949.
9. Speech delivered at the Paris Peace Conference, April 1949 (Paul Robeson Collection).
10. Speech delivered at welcome-home rally, Rockland Palace, Harlem, June 19, 1949 (Paul Robeson Collection).
11. Speech delivered at rally to free the Trenton Six, sponsored by the Civil Rights Congress, Newark, July 24, 1949.
12. Howard Fast, *Peekskill, U.S.A.* (New York: Civil Rights Congress, 1951).
13. Ibid.
14. Ibid.
15. Eleanor Roosevelt, quoted in Seton, *Paul Robeson*.
16. Interview with Dan Burley, *New York Age*, August/September 1949.
17. Ibid.
18. Quoted in Seton, *Paul Robeson*.
19. Ibid.
20. *New York Herald Tribune*, editorial, August 6, 1950.
21. From petition, "We Charge Genocide" (Paul Robeson Collection).
22. Paul Robeson, *Here I Stand* (New York: Othello Associates, 1957).
23. From testimony before HUAC (Paul Robeson Collection).
24. Paul Robeson, *Here I Stand*.
25. Ibid.

CHAPTER 6

1. Paul Robeson, *Here I Stand* (New York: Othello Associates, 1957).
2. Statement to press, August 1964 (Paul Robeson Collection).
3. Last public statement—tape-recorded message presented at salute to Paul Robeson, Carnegie Hall, April 26, 1973 (Paul Robeson Collection).